Praise For *Farang*

'Ripper yarns with an Asian twist—focused wit and original wisdom from the Doc who has done most things, all successfully.'
- John Weinthal, Writer and Broadcaster, Kuala Lumpur

'Not only does Dr Iain see the things that make up Thailand, but he experiences them as well, bringing up unseen aspects and presenting them to the reader in a very humorous way.'
- Lang Reid, *Chiangmai Mail*

'Like all good doctors and authors, Dr Iain Corness provides comfort for the aches and pains of ex-pat life. He chronicles the frustration and misunderstandings that go hand in hand with applying for a house loan, to getting married or buried, illustrating them in a series of delightful and insightful stories that will amuse, inform and stimulate anyone who has ever travelled to or settled down to live in Thailand. Finding the right balance between your own values and adapting to those in a foreign land is never easy, but the good doctor has written a prescription that is not hard to swallow: it requires a large dollop of humour mixed with a portion of patience, and a teaspoon of goodwill. Having read the stories, I am feeling better already.'
- Christopher G. Moore, author of the critically acclaimed and best-selling *Land of Sunshine* trilogy

'If anyone was equipped to write a series of short stories on life in Thailand from the perspective of the *farang*, it must surely be Dr Iain Corness. No detail of Thai life—big or small—escapes the good doctor's microscopic examination in his wickedly funny musings on ex-pat life. What makes his stories so compelling is his gentle understanding and good humour, recounting examples of the idiosyncrasies and frustrations faced and felt by many western visitors when they first come to Thailand. I could not stop laughing or nodding in agreement as I enjoyed his delightful and insightful stories.'

- Gary Stubbs, *Queensland Business Acumen* magazine

'This book highlights so many of the wonderful differences of living as an ex-pat. Dr Iain Corness, the *farang* in this book, takes you through these differences with a self deprecating humour, but you can see yourself in the same situations. A genuinely insightful look at our lives, portrayed in a very witty fashion.'

- Graham Macdonald, Vice-Chairman, British Chamber of Commerce, Thailand

FARANG

FARANG

DR IAIN CORNESS

maverick house

Every effort has been made to contact the copyright holders of material reproduced in this text. In cases where these efforts have been unsuccessful, the copyright holders are asked to contact the publishers directly.

PUBLISHED BY MAVERICK HOUSE PUBLISHERS.

Maverick House Publishers, 47 Harrington Street, Dublin 8, Ireland.

info@maverickhouse.com
http://www.maverickhouse.com

ISBN: 978-1-905379-42-2

5 4

The paper used in this book comes from wood pulp of managed forests. For every tree felled, at least one tree is planted, thereby renewing natural resources.

A CIP catalogue record for this book is available from the British Library.

Dedication

This book is dedicated to my late father and wonderfully very alive mother, who made me look at life enquiringly; and to my delightful Thai wife Som, who never ceases to be amazed at all the 'normal' things in Thailand which amaze me!

Acknowledgements

How do you, with one's first book, thank everyone who made it possible?

Perhaps I should start with a succession of English teachers who managed, all those years ago, to impart a smattering of interest in the English language? Alas, their names have gone with the passing of time, but they are not forgotten.

It appears customary to thank one's spouse, and I see no reason to break that custom. My Thai wife, the delightful Som, has been the inspiration for many of the tales in this book, even though at the time she did not realise it. The cobra in the kitchen story belongs to her. I only recorded the aftermath. She opened a door not just to a cobra, but to the culture of Thailand, that I could never have opened on my own. If it were not for her, I would still be standing outside barbershops on Wednesdays, blissfully unaware of the midweek superstitions.

Of course, there are many people who have a book in their minds, as yet unwritten. Mine too could have been gestational or worse, stillborn, if it were not for the publishers, or dare I say, 'my publishers' at Maverick House. Some of the staff I have met, such as John Mooney who brought my contract to Thailand. He probably still does not believe that I didn't really understand it, but his explanation that 'It's a standard publisher's contract' was all I needed. I signed, and on that day felt that I was becoming 'a writer'.

Another I have met, who has amazed me with his eye for detail, is Pornchai Sereemongkonpol, who would ring me to let me know I had gotten confused with the kryptonite item, and that they hadn't made a sequel to the *Top Gun* movie (read on; all will become clear). So if you find some errors of fact after all that, I'll let you blame Pornchai, rather than me! Thank you Khun Pornchai.

The third person I met from the publishers was Jean Harrington, who replied in such good grace when I asked her what her part in the organisation was. 'I am the managing director,' she said so sweetly, while I cringed with embarrassment! Thank you, Jean for your encouragement.

The final three I have not met, but I owe them all a debt of gratitude. The first is Adam Hyland, who has been my editor over there in Ireland, and who had the unenviable job of making 60 short stories into a 'book'. I thank you. Secondly Gert Ackermann, who has masterminded the publicity for my humble first book, all done from afar. And finally, Sarah Ormston, who appeared only in my email inbox but enthused, encouraged and prodded, and had me spending nights writing, to fulfil her expectations as to the number of words needed. It was Sarah who alerted me to the Maverick House website (www.maverickhouse.com) and the 'forthcoming titles' page, where in June I saw the cover and a description of this book. It was at that point I went from being 'a writer' to being 'an author'—in my own mind at least. Thank you Sarah.

Of course there are always others who have helped in some way or another, such as Peter Malhotra (MD of the *Pattaya Mail*) who helped lift me up any time I fell over in Thailand (and there were a few stumbles), and I also thank my eldest son, Dr Jonathan Corness, who has been just so enthusiastic, and made me feel that it was worthwhile pursuing my dream.

This book, my book, is also yours. Thank you.

Preface

I have known Iain Corness for over 40 years, from his days as a penniless medical student through to today. Despite everything, he did graduate and is a real medical doctor.

He was born in the UK but emigrated, as an early teenager, with his family to Australia—the land of his upbringing.

This upbringing was a relatively conventional one, but conventional he is not.

Over time he has had four wives, fathered four boys and a daughter, raced and built competition cars, owned a Thai restaurant, operated his own professional photographic studio and much more, all the while doctoring, mainly in Brisbane, Australia.

Relocation to Thailand in the mid-1990s was supposedly leading to an early retirement, but the need for funds led to his writing for the English language weekly *Pattaya Mail* newspaper, while also acting as a consultant for the International Department of the Bangkok Hospital Pattaya.

The Good Doc, as he likes to be known, is almost excessively competitive, enthusiastic, energetic and imaginative. He can also be extremely witty and insightful. Each of these characteristics is evident in the book you are now holding.

It is unlikely that any other person anywhere produces six wholly informative and entertaining columns a week on six different subjects: Medicine, Motoring, Dining Out, a Book Review, Photography and another 'secret' literary assignment. Check out the *Pattaya Mail* on the internet—it's all there every week.

Corness is unique, and this book showcases some of the talent of this extraordinary character.

- John Weinthal, Writer and Broadcaster,
Kuala Lumpur

Introduction

Dear Reader,

By purchasing this book you will have assisted two young children with their education: Young Miss Marisa and even younger Master Evan. My children! Education in Thailand is expensive.

So right from the outset, you can see that basic honesty and truths will be revealed to you in this book. I wrote it because I need the money.

It is a small volume covering my experiences as a foreigner in an alien culture. After you have lived in a foreign country for a while, all the 'amazing' differences between it and your own society eventually seem to disappear as you become inured and hardened in your new environment.

I began writing these short stories to keep alive the fascination for something new, and then realised that they might also be of interest to others who were either living here in Thailand, had visited the Kingdom, or were maybe even contemplating living here.

They deliberately do not follow a sequence, because I wanted to convey the random and fleeting thoughts that living in Thailand can inspire in anybody who comes to this wonderful place.

However, they are all factual—even ones like the cobra in the kitchen, which still gives my wife nightmares, and the epic plane trip punctuated by vomiting by my young daughter, but it's alright, we'll never fly that airline again!

And I suggest that you don't either. And beware of sticky blankets.

Anyone who has visited Thailand will relate to the story of my first Thai meal, and those who have sneaked away for a couple of hours of dalliance will recognise the soapy saga of the Mogambo (unfortunately torn down to make a freeway or something equally as unexciting).

One thing you should glean from these items is that for me, Thailand remains the most exciting and endearing country I have ever lived and worked in. It has its frustrations, as you will read in the item on getting married, or on getting a passport for my daughter, but the hilarity that stems from everyday living is still there.

I am living in the country that other people work and save for 11 months, just to spend four weeks over here. No wonder I am known to break out into spontaneous laughter, for no apparent reason.

However, by the time you have finished this small book, you will at least appreciate a few of those reasons!

I hope you enjoy it, and my children will thank you for buying it!

- Iain Corness, Pattaya, Thailand, 2007.

Above: The spirit house supermarket, if you can believe there is such a thing. I soon found out that one spirit house was not enough; I needed one 'one leg' and one 'four leg' house. But of course!

Right: The Thai-style garden gnomes I was also expected to buy.

My Spirit Houses

IT WAS A FEW YEARS ago now, but one of those times in my life when something had to change. I am sure you have all experienced them too. Perhaps a mid-life crisis, or maybe something less dramatic, but a turning point if nothing else.

My wife of countless years had gone back to Australia to 'find herself', but found an American architect instead, and was now living in the US. So I was divorced, living alone and probably feeling a trifle sorry for myself.

One evening, while surveying my street, I suddenly saw a difference between my house and all the others. They all had spirit houses! Or *San Phra Poom* as Thai people call them. 'Ah Ha!' I said to myself, I have probably offended the spirits by not offering them an abode. That was why things were turning pear-shaped for me. I would change that and change my life at the same time. Having made the decision, I got another beer from the fridge. You cannot change everything in one's life too quickly.

Of course, I am not the only *farang* to have noticed the beauty of spirit houses, and become fascinated by them. In 2003, David Beckham, with his wife Victoria in tow, bought no less than six spirit houses from a roadside shop. According to reports, they were for decorative rather than spiritual purposes. But then, there's not much wrong with their lives these days, so it looks like their purchases have served them well.

The next day I went to a spirit house shop on Sukhumvit Road, a place that had hundreds of them lined up in all styles and colours. It was a veritable celestial housing estate. Unfortunately I was unable to get the message across that I wanted to purchase one, which seemed a strange outcome not imagined when you enter a shop, so I left empty-handed. The spirits, it seemed, were not yet with me.

When you come up against a brick wall in Thailand, I have always found there is a font of all knowledge close by. This font is generally called 'the maid'. Patiently it was explained to me that you didn't just plop one of these celestial bungalows in the front yard. It required the services of a monk. At that stage, in retrospect, I should have backed out, but by now I was all fired up with enthusiasm to join the spiritual community of my street.

There is a temple two kilometres from my house, and with my maid in tow I presented myself to a saffron-robed elderly gentleman, to be told that I was addressing the wrong type of monk. I needed a Brahmin for this job. Unfortunately it seemed that Brahmins were a little scarce.

I may have looked despondent at this latest turn of events, but not my maid, who informed me that any old person would do (me excluded, of course). She had just the person—an old crone in my street who nodded sagely and dictated a shopping list, which appeared to have more items on it than the Pattaya Orphanage's Saturday supermarket shopping spree.

The spirit house supermarket was in Naklua in Chonburi, where a smiling young man helped load my spiritual shopping trolley. We had a group of small people, a pair of horses, elephants, three different bolts of material, a strange pair of umbrella-looking things, incense sticks and fairy lights. Only 1,540 baht later and I had what I presumed was the necessary doings to keep even the grumpiest of spirits in good humour and well housed.

However, it appeared we needed someone to position said spirit house, but fortunately, the spirit house outfitters did a comprehensive service and a suitably ascetic looking gentleman was produced to do the honours.

I arrived home, rather proud of the accomplishments so far, to be regaled by a hand-wringing maid. What was wrong now? Amid entreaties and entangled English she said I needed more than one spirit house—I needed two! In my innocence I had not seen that the spirits were into property development! However, I agreed immediately. Silly me! Of course we needed two spirit houses!

I picked up Khun Ascetic, with a string of jade beads around his neck, a compass and a spirit level (only as I typed that, did I realise just how apt). Waving a pointed stick in the air, which had a bell at one end, he awaited divine inspiration, which came with much bell ringing and spearing of the stick into the ground. This was done several times and finally all the co-ordinates were joined to give the site for the spiritual residences.

Now came the sales pitch. My ascetic could take away all the worries and cares from my shoulders and he would arrange for the two spirit houses, one of which was called 'one leg' and the other which was called 'four legs' and would have the plinth built, residences erected, suitable incantations, the whole shooting match. And it would only cost 30,000 baht!

At that rate, I reckoned the spirits would be living better than I, and was going to suggest for that money, the spirits just take over the main house and I'd live in 'one leg' or 'four leg'. I begged off. Sometimes it is good to be unable to speak Thai!

I returned to the office to be met by my secretary, babbling, 'I speak with your maid, we can fix spirit houses and only cost 10-12,000 baht.' How could I refuse such a spiritual bargain?

We repaired to the purveyors of spirit houses on Sukhumvit. Suitable one leg and four legs were selected and paid for: 3,700 baht, delivery included! Another bargain.

Next was the Officiating Person for the installation who turned out to be the requisite Brahmin. He looked at the co-ordinates left by Khun Ascetic, modified them slightly, and we were almost there!

It was decided that 11 July was auspicious, and the whole ceremony could begin at 7am. Promptly at 7am (now there's a first!) the secretary and the Officiating Brahmin, now all dressed in white, arrived at the house. Figurines were unwrapped, small horses, elephants, and incense holders put in position, while the maid laid a groaning table in front of the houses. One factor was certain—these spirits were not going to go hungry that Thursday morning.

Incantations ensued, but then I found I was part of the proceedings too, having to place incense sticks in an urn while asking for the spirits to smile upon the main house and myself. I suddenly found myself very moved and humbled by this situation. I felt honoured and touched. Tears started to well up in my eyes—it was a very emotional moment.

So now my house was complete with its two spirit houses. I have done my bit to keep them fed, watered and amused in return for some spiritual assistance. I feel I probably need their help more than they need mine, but I do my best in my clumsy, stumbling *farang* way. I'm sure they'll understand.

~

Tales of a Thai Kitchen

I LIVE IN A SMALL house with a Thai kitchen, which is not surprising because the small house is also Thai. When the kitchen was built at the rear of the house, it had been open to the elements, as most Thai kitchens tend to be, but successive owners had seen to it being enclosed and roofed in, while I had a door put in the new rear wall. This back door went nowhere, other than into scrubland, but at least we had a choice of exits in case of emergency. I was not to know I had just set the scene for one.

One evening I rang home to tell my wife I was running a trifle late, but instead of her carefully modulated tones, designating a non-native English speaker, I was assailed by rapid and voluble Thai, so loud that the phone was hardly necessary. This was my maid, whose command of English is only slightly better than my ability in Tagalog, a language in which I can say 'I love you' and nothing else. Mind you, that's enough to get you into some interesting sitcoms, and those who would like to know other magic words in assorted languages can contact me care of the publisher.

I am sure you have also been in these lack-of-common-language situations. In one hand you have a phone with Thai words cascading from it, and all around you is emptiness. Not a Thai speaker in sight. Shouting, 'Sak kroo, sak kroo,' (wait, wait) at the phone, I ran around till I finally found someone who could converse with the by now hysterical maid.

It apparently only took a few seconds for my phone interpreter to get the gist of what was happening, and he suggested I should return home immediately as we had a problem in the house.

'What problem?' I shouted.

'In kitchen,' was the inscrutable reply.

I drove quickly back home, wondering what could be the problem that was so great that my wife could not answer the phone and would cause the maid to go hysterical. As I pulled up at the front, it indeed started to look ominous. A 'song taew' taxi bus was outside, along with the maid's motorcycle, a police pickup and a van from the zoo. How could all these disparate items come together?

Rushing inside, I was met by the maid, who started at fever pitch and 40 megawatts again. However, there were others in the front room who looked more of a threat; two policemen with drawn side arms and a scruffy looking gent wearing the shirt of the local taxi company. I had by now found the owner/drivers/

occupants of three of the four vehicles outside my gate. All that was missing was the zookeeper. Zookeeper? Was this some strange nightmare?

I did not have to wait long for the answer, as a swarthy chap emerged from the kitchen holding a canvas bag that contained some type of very alive, wriggling livestock. Now all were accounted for, other than my wife, who then opened the bedroom door about 3 cms, asking if he had 'got it?'

'Got what?'

'The snake!'

'Ah!'

With the state of emergency over, I sat down with my wife, who pieced together the saga. The emergency had apparently begun around an hour before, when my wife had gone into the kitchen to make some dinner. She opened the cupboard under the sink to grab the wok and suddenly found she was looking into the eyes of a cobra, which reared up, hood extended. The cupboard door was quickly slammed shut and she ran to phone me, but my phone rang through. She then rang the maid, who lived only 500 metres up the street, who came down on her motorcycle. Deciding that none of her brooms and whisks would do the job, she went back and dragged down the taxi driver who lived next door. However, the taxi driver was savvy, as he knew that cobras do not hire taxis, so he suggested that they should call the police. This they did.

The police pickup arrived, complete with two policemen from the finest police force that money can buy (if one believes all one can read in the popular press). Guns drawn, they approached the kitchen cupboards, but then stopped and explained that all they could do was shoot the snake, and that might bring bad karma down for everyone. It was time for a rethink.

The zoo! Unfortunately, nobody knew the telephone number, so the taxi driver set off to fetch the snake man. In the meantime, my wife, unsure that two loaded police .38s were sufficient protection from a now very disturbed and probably very disgruntled cobra, decided to barricade herself in the bedroom.

After 30 minutes, the cabbie arrived back, with the snake catcher in his van close behind. Snake catcher knew his stuff and very quickly picked up the cobra and placed it in his sack. The emergency was now over, at which point I had arrived back in my house.

However, in Thailand there is another small matter to be dealt with. This was the part that was to really involve me. The small matter of payment! With much 'sotto voce' mutterings between my wife and the maid, whilst the policemen, the taxi driver and the snake catcher stood around looking at the floor, it was decided that cabbie should get 100 baht, the policemen 200 baht between them and the snake catcher 400 baht. After my wallet was 700 baht lighter and everyone was smiling, the players in the mini-drama left.

I wonder if the snake got to see any of that money.

~

My First Thai Meal

IT WAS MANY YEARS AGO, in fact 31 this year, when I was first introduced to Thai cuisine. What I was doing in Thailand is almost worth a page on its own, as I had absolutely no knowledge of the Kingdom, and two days before I arrived I was still unsure about coming over.

I have a friend, an Aussie, who was involved in setting up factories in Thailand for his Australian company. He had been over three times previously, but was no authority on Thai food; in fact, he would only eat unpeeled bananas, as that was sustenance that nobody had managed to touch. The current 'Clean food-Good taste' promotion for anxious tourists had not been thought of in those days.

I had just gone through a divorce, had not had a holiday for seven years, and was dangerously close to burnout. My friend could see this (in fact everyone could, other than me), and he suggested I come with him to Thailand for a two-week vacation. I vacillated (a lovely word for being unable to make up your mind), but finally on the Friday said I would go if there was a seat on the plane. He was going on the Saturday.

Somehow he produced a plane ticket and I spent the rest of Friday getting double doses of all the required vaccinations that were mandatory in those days. I was no stranger to travel, having spent three years in Europe and the UK, but I certainly was a stranger to Thailand, and its cuisine. So now that sets the backdrop for my first Thai meal.

We went into the reasonably clean-looking restaurant in our hotel, as he had decided that having his doctor mate with him, he might try something other than bananas! We sat down and the menu was brought to the table.

Being a hotel with delusions of grandeur, the menu was written in English on one page, and in Thai script on the other. However, I had already noticed that the English section covered European choices, and the Thai section, though written in Thai, (a script that still defies me), did not seem to be the equivalent of the European sections on the facing page. There were more of the items to each section, and so I deduced this was genuine Thai cuisine that lay hidden in the hieroglyphs. I asked the attendant waiter: 'This Thai food?' pointing to the Thai page.

'Yes sir,' was the smiling reply.

Now being time to order, my friend Aussie the Brave ordered steak with eggs and potato, while I berated him for being such a stick-in-the-mud. 'You're in Thailand, you should eat Thai!'

Having duly chastised him, I perused the unknowns on the Thai menu, and after deciding that the main courses had to be somewhere in the middle of the page, confidently pointed out one item to the waiter. At that point I was quite sure I had cracked the Da Vinci code when the waiter nodded with obvious approval and scurried off with our orders.

In due course our food arrived. My friend's looked as you would expect of a Thai chef having a crack at European cooking, all those years ago. The steak was small and shrivelled, the eggs runny and greasy and the potato turned out to be soggy chips.

On the other hand, mine was magnificent—pure white fluffy rice beside a stir-fried dish of thin bite-sized pieces of meat, done in some type of sauce with small chopped pieces of shallot all over the top. I smiled outwardly at my perspicacity, while the waiters (there were now three at my elbow, which should have been a warning) also smiled outwardly.

We began. My friend's steak and eggs were not the best, but also not the worst he had eaten, said he, and it certainly beat bananas.

Meanwhile I began my stir-fried steak and shallots, but after the first mouthful I knew it was not shallots. It was something that held more fire potential than anything I had ever held in my mouth this side of petrol.

I kept smiling, being too proud to admit that perhaps my initial foray into Thai food was perhaps a little too adventurous. My tongue was on fire, sweat was starting to run out of my hair and into my eyebrows.

I began drinking glasses of iced water, with one waiter now fully occupied with the task of refilling the water jug. I tried keeping ice cubes in my mouth and wrapping my tongue around them. All to no avail.

Finally the first waiter came over. 'Is it a little too spicy for you, sir?' I nodded, as by now my tongue felt as if it were three times its normal size and speech was beyond me. 'Water does not help, sir,' he said. 'What you need is sugar,' bringing me over a sugar bowl.

Almost in tears by this stage, I began shovelling sugar into my mouth and washing it down with the iced water.

'No, sir, you leave it on your tongue,' said my helpful waiter. By this stage I would have poured it in my ear if he had told me to, as he was my only hope of salvation. My friend was laughing so much at his red-faced dining companion that he almost choked too.

Of course, all Thai food old hands will realise that the dish I had so confidently chosen did not come with chopped shallots, but those small fiery chillies, known as *'prik khee noo,'* or in the vernacular, 'mouse shit peppers'. The hottest chilli in the Thai kitchen!

My tongue did settle eventually, and many years later in my life when I actually owned a Thai restaurant, the chefs showed me how they 'balance' the fire in any Thai dish with sugar. But I have never forgotten *prik khee noo* (bird chilli) and my first steps in Thai cuisine! Nor the lesson I learned for trying to be smart.

~

You Want Go Mogambo?

It was with those fateful words, 'You want go Mogambo, Boss?' that I was inducted into the sudsy, seedy underbelly of Thai massage, 30 years ago.

It was 1975, but the memory still burns brightly in the dark hidden recesses of my mind. This was when I had been brought over to Thailand by my friend. He was rather well versed in the mystic East, and was happy to show me the delights on offer to help me get over my traumatic divorce.

We stayed at the Ambassador Hotel on Sukhumvit Soi 11, but it was very different then, compared to today. It was very modest, down a narrow lane from the two lane concrete strip, with dirt verges on both sides that was Sukhumvit. The traffic was such that you could actually walk across the road without checking on your whole-of-life coverage beforehand. There was a string of taxis that used to live in Soi 11, and the Datsun Bluebird 1200 was universal. 'My' driver was a smiling chap by the name of Sawang, who could at least speak a little English.

On the second afternoon, my friend said he would show me something of the city. Sawang leapt to attention as we came down the Ambassador's steps, and with my friend in the front and me in the rear, we set off. I never asked where we were going, as I didn't know Bangkok, but I knew he had the experience.

We swung into a large car park in front of an imposing building. We got out and walked towards the liveried commissionaires who opened the doors with a flourish. I presumed we were going to meet somebody in this establishment, and I also presumed it was a hotel. I was correct with the first presumption, and totally wrong with the second.

We moved through the foyer and there in front of me was the most incredible sight. Behind a glass wall were scores of the most gorgeous women I had ever clapped eyes on. They were sitting on carpeted tiers, dressed in evening gowns, complete with handbags. My brain went into overdrive. This was 2pm. What was happening?

A young Thai man, whom I have always subsequently referred to as the Maitre d' approached and asked if I had been there before. I weakly said no. He then said in a conspiratorial whisper, 'The ladies on the left are for the hand massage, the ladies on the right are for the body massage.'

To demonstrate my total naïvetè, I asked why anyone would want their hands massaged. 'No sir, the ladies on the left massage you with their hands. The ladies on the right massage you with their bodies.'

My ensuing indecision was made up for by the alacrity of my old mate, who said, 'He'll have a body massage.'

The Maitre d' sidled up again, asking, 'What number would you like, sir?'

I began stammering, something I hadn't done since childhood, as 100 pairs of brown eyes honed in on me.

'What's your room number at the Ambassador?' asked my friend.

'93,' I replied, and seconds later the Maitre d' was on a microphone calling out, '93', and nano-seconds later, a gorgeous young lady, complete with evening dress and handbag and a Number 93 badge was making her way towards me.

The next minute or two were a blur as I was escorted upstairs and into a two-room 'apartment' where I was seated and asked if I wanted a beer. I most certainly did, as I had no idea what was next, and very quickly another young girl (the apprentice) appeared with my beer and then began filling a rather large bath in the other room.

In the meantime, Number 93 deftly slipped out of her dress and wrapped herself in a towel, right in front of me, and I swear to this day, I saw nothing! She then motioned that I should undress too. Deft was not an adjective I would have applied to myself. Deeply embarrassed would be more accurate, but by the time I was down to the pink one-button, I was taken into the 'bath' room and immersed.

With the water lapping around my pink ears, I then received the best bathing I had experienced since I was six months old and my mother was doing the honours. I was squeaky clean—everywhere!

Meanwhile, the apprentice was soaping up a large inflatable Li-Lo mattress, and then tactfully withdrew. Number 93 hauled me up from the bath and indicated I should lie down on Li-Lo. This I did, modestly face down, and my 'body massage' began.

To say the experience was 'sensual' is an understatement. Very soon I began to worry that I was going to puncture the Li-Lo, but was then smartly whipped over on to my back for the second half. You could have flown the Australian flag from my appendage by this stage, but Number 93 ignored it all, gliding and sliding past Willie the Wonder Wand as if it were not there!

Unnoticed by me, the apprentice had returned and refilled the bath, and flagpole and I were immersed once more, until we were again both squeaky clean. Number 93 then indicated that I could lie down on the bed in the other room, but I was far too scared. Honestly!

I dressed, tipped heavily and ran out to Sawang and the waiting taxi. I was speechless, but my friend was laughing. 'That's Mogambo,' he said.

The next day, I came out of the hotel after lunch and was immediately pounced upon by a grinning Sawang.

'You want go Mogambo, Boss?' he asked. Did I? But that, of course, is another story for another day!

By the way, before you go looking for the Mogambo Turkish bath house (commonly known to Thais as *ab ob naud*) it was knocked down many years ago—but there are others happily splashing around today!

~

The New Maid

HAVING COME FROM AUSTRALIA, I thought it was impossible to employ a maid. Domestic help was far too expensive an item, even for middle-upper income earners such as myself. Then there was the nightmare of inviting unionism into the home, with its 37½ hour week, four weeks holiday with pay, plus 17.5% holiday loading, compulsory superannuation, health benefits— do you want me to go on? So to come to Thailand, a country where even the maids have maids, this had the potential to be truly the paradise of which dreams are made. (Sorry about the pun.)

As 'newbies' when we first arrived, my now ex-wife and I marvelled at the fact that we did not even have to advertise for our maid. A young woman just appeared at the door and in very halting English explained that she would work for us as a maid. We were made! (Sorry about that pun again.) And indeed she did appear for some several weeks, but then disappeared with my wife's gold necklace and assorted cash. We had much to learn about this 'maid' business.

The next maid came with a recommendation from an ex-pat family going home, and she was a little diamond. Unfortunately, like many diamonds in Thailand, she turned out to be a cubic zirconium when left to her own devices. The UBC satellite TV stations held a much greater attraction than the washing machine. And the whiskey appeared to suffer badly with evaporation in the hot days of summer. But better the devil you know than one you don't. We endured—at least the floors were swept and the clothes ironed, but when my then wife gave up work and stayed at home, the maid did the same.

Maid number three was also another recommendation from an ex-pat family. The fact that they were *NOT* going home should have been a warning, but we were there for the plucking. And we were nicely de-feathered. We had been sold a lemon.

This woman will always be memorable for the fact that she was totally as thick as two short planks. Forget about teaching old dogs new tricks; this woman defied belief. She had her way of doing things, even if it meant beating the wet clothes on the top of the washing machine, rather than putting them inside it and turning it on. She had never heard of the industrial revolution and certainly wasn't going to play any part in it!

However, after several months she mastered the art of turning on the TV, and housework was sacrificed on the altar of UBC. I cancelled UBC and she resigned.

So to maid number four. Having found that getting recommendations from ex-pat families was akin to getting your estranged wife's solicitor to act for you as well, in an acrimonious contested divorce action, I changed tactics. Recommendations for a maid should come from another maid, I reasoned.

I asked the maid employed in the office to find me a maid. This she did, though it did cost me 1,000 baht finder's fee!

Number four was a hill tribe lady, who spoke a little Thai and even less English, but what she lacked in linguistic skills, she made up for in superstitions. When I suggested that I wanted to get a spirit house for my residence this brought much wailing and hand wringing. It was she who insisted that I had to have two, which I managed to find out through the use of interpreters.

I persevered and two spirit houses were consecrated, or whatever one does with spirit houses. On certain days of the month, the maid would arrive with 'sacrifices' at odd hours of the morning, and chanting and burning of paper would ensue. The pigs' heads that I found scattered around from time to time appeared to have been severed before arriving at the house, but sometimes I wondered.

The demise of maid number four was brought about by a combination of jealousy and presbyopia (the short-sightedness brought on by aging). By this stage, my maid had only me to worry about, as my *farang* wife had by now decided to 'do' for herself and took everything to Australia, but did send up the divorce papers for me to sign.

My maid would make my breakfast and have little else to do for the rest of the day, but the plethora of stations on the local cable TV made up for the lack of work. A sort of balance was reached. However, this was upset with the advent of my new lady friend after about one year. Never mind the problems with having two women in one kitchen. Two women in one house was enough.

The maid began attempting to undermine the intruder. 'I think she have boyfriend Thai,' was ploy number one. 'Forgetting' to do my lady's underfripperies was number two. Suggesting to my lady that I did not like what she was cooking for me was number three.

But my lady was not going to be overrun by a nomadic hill tribe person. She began pointing out what the short-sighted maid (in many ways) was missing while cleaning the house. The end was nigh. The end cost money (mine of course), but at least there was no undercurrent in the household. But there was also no maid, and my lady was now my wife and a little bundle of joy was expected the next year! What would I do this time?

The recommendation for maid number five came from my new wife's mother. A mature-aged lady from the same village as my wife's family got the nod. She would live in and double as Nanny, and has so far managed to outlast the others, even if she does also manage to make herself busy cleaning everywhere I want to be.

She is attempting to wash the floor under my chair as I type—so I must finish here. Wish me luck!

~

Getting Married

WE ALL HAVE AN ACQUAINTANCE who knows everything that it is necessary to know to live successfully as an expat in Thailand. That acquaintance for me has lived here for 20 years, dresses in tie-dye drawstring trousers and wears a T-shirt that says Singha Beer, or Carlsberg, or Chang or Beer Lao or ... but you get the picture. Hardly the epitome of sartorial elegance, but he's 'been here for 20 years' so we all give him and others like him the respect that is owed to long time stayers. That respect can be misplaced.

The last time I listened to one of these fonts of all knowledge was when I was planning to get married to my Thai sweetheart. I mentioned, within the hearing of the tie-dye drawstring-trousered font that I would have to find out what was required.

'It's simple,' said tie-dye, 'just pop down to the *amphur* (local government office). They do it on the spot.'

Chuffed by this, my lady and I made a date to go to the local *amphur*. 'Should I wear a jacket?' was my biggest worry, so deciding that it was better to be overdressed with jacket and tie, we drove to the local *amphur* office.

Now for those who have never been to the *amphur*, let me describe this noble institution of Thai legal formalities. Expense was definitely spared on the construction, and grey paint was obviously cheaper than other more friendly hues. It was a fine example of what you get when the lowest tender gets the contract.

The *amphur* also attracts people of all ages who congregate around the entrance, as well as the ice cream sellers and assorted cooks of Thai delicacies. Inside, the uniformed government people seem to walk past purposefully, but since they return to walk past several times, one begins to doubt the importance of the purpose.

However, we did know what we wanted. We had popped down to the *amphur* because we wanted to get married.

Entering the foyer area, we moved towards the enquiry counter, but before we could ask, the tired gentleman who had obviously seen everything before said, 'Marry?' and pointed to a door on the right.

We entered another area, similar to a bank, with 'tellers' windows and rows of seats for those waiting. There were many waiting. This should have been an omen, but we were in love and were excited. There was also one of those, by now almost universal, numbered ticket dispensers.

We sat quietly together with ticket 407, wondering if there was time to have a pee before we were called to the nuptial window. We both decided to hold on. This was to be an important moment in our lives, and we certainly did not wish to miss wedding ticket 407 being called to the window by a call of nature!

We were finally given the call and eagerly sat down before a formidable lady in a brown suit. I was relying on my bride to tell me when I had to reply to the, 'Do you take this woman ...?' as my Thai is minimal. With much waving of arms we were given instead, a small piece of paper with 'For Foreigner' on the top, with six different clauses, all in Thai, other than the words 'Permission Book'. We were dismissed and Lucky Number 408 was called.

Were we married yet? 'Don't we have to sign anything?' I said, showing the inherent naivety of the ex-pat without enough Thai language skills.

'Not yet,' said wife-to-be, 'we have to get the Permission Book first.'

Silly me, sitting there in jacket and tie with my passport in the pocket. Of course we'd need a Permission Book! What the hell was a Permission Book?

A trip up to the British Embassy in Bangkok revealed that the 'book' was in fact an affirmation by me that I was entitled to marry and not about to commit bigamy. There was no book, it was just a form, but one that you have to type out yourself, not one that you filled out.

The reason for this is still unknown to me, but perhaps an embassy person reading this can fill me in on this point?

Having typed out your affirmation, you then go back to the embassy complete with passport and original copies of divorce papers or death certificates of any previous spouse.

'Copies will not be accepted under any circumstances!' say the guidance notes from the British Embassy. You have been warned. You also have to pay a couple of thousand baht, or so, to get someone there to witness your signature, all of which takes two days.

The fun now begins in earnest. You have to get the witnessed affirmation translated into Thai, by an official translation agency, and stamped by them. Ready to pop down to the *amphur* yet? Not so fast, young man. You have to get the affirmation and the translation certified by the Legalisation and Naturalisation Division, Department of Consular Affairs, Ministry of Foreign Affairs, and that's in Chaeng Wattana, so it's back to Bangers!

Take along two photocopies of everything you can possibly think of, including your puppy's immunisation record, and practice *'jai yen yen'*. Eventually, after you have been told to wait, add this, write that, and so on, you will get the documents back. Up to two full days later, I am told, but you can circumvent this by paying extra. I paid.

But don't get the suit out of the wardrobe just yet— there's more! You need a letter from the Immigration

Police, verifying your place of abode. This is mercifully quick and costs a miserly 300 baht, a veritable bargain.

Again visit the photocopier and get two copies of everything, including the pages in your passport with your TM immigration card, sign the lot till you have writer's cramp, and then, finally, you can 'just pop down to the *amphur*,' as my friend called it. Smile sweetly and you are certified as man and wife. Simple really. Just like the man said!

~

Child Raising Made Easy

THE HEADING IS ERRONEOUS. IT should read 'Child raising made easier,' as no matter where, what, why and with whom, child raising is never easy, so I apologise in advance if you feel you have been conned into reading this item under false pretences.

Mind you, I do firmly believe that all writers should have some bona fides as regards their subjects, before assuming the active hunched keyboard position and galloping into print. Gentle reader, I have served my apprenticeship in child rearing. I most certainly have.

Apart from the fact that I am a graduate physician, who has had his fair share of paediatric cases ('pediatric' if you come from the left hand side of the Atlantic Ocean), I have also had (more than) my fair share of children to raise. Five at last count, with my eldest son being 33 years old and my youngest son 11 months. I do hasten to add that this does not qualify me for an expert's badge or world champion progenitor certificate, but you have to agree, it makes me definitely well experienced!

Having expressed my suitability to write on this subject, I must also say that I am in the position to compare the act of child raising between the Western world and Thailand. Current score; three fifths in the west and two fifths over here.

For this to be a proper scientific study however, all other factors should have remained the same, and I must shamefully admit there are some differences, or complicating factors. I have grown older for one, and the last two fifths have a different mother (but same father, I assure you). I have rather peculiar ears, and when people first meet me they often ask if I did a lot of boxing, or was the hooker in the rugby scrum for my school team. My youngest son and daughter also possess a pair each of these auricular appendages, so DNA testing was decided to be unnecessary for either.

Enough preamble to this study in comparative child rearing—let's get down to the nitty-gritty of it all. Think back to when you were awaiting the advent of child number 1 in the Western world. Together with your spouse, you went on a buying spree. Posters of rabbits and ducks for the walls of the baby's room, the cot with spinning things on the ends, a mobile made of swans and other nursery animals to hang from the ceiling, and the *pièce de résistance*—the electronic alarm, which connected to the master bedroom so that baby's cries could be heard in the middle of the night.

You probably even felt very paternal/maternal (delete whichever inappropriate) doing the best for the yet unborn offspring. You were showing just how responsible you were with the forthcoming parenthood. You weren't. You had fallen into the Western trap. I shall explain later.

Now we come to the Thailand scenario. While awaiting the arrival of my first Thai offspring, I began to get anxious when my Thai wife kept putting off my suggestions regarding the bunnies on the wall, cot and other paraphernalia. As 'explosion' date loomed closer, I again proposed we go shopping for the cot without delay, to be told that a cot wasn't necessary, as baby would sleep with us in the bed!

'Is this what happens in Thailand?' I asked incredulously.

'Yes, darling, baby sleeps between us,' was the reply. I expressed my misgivings, but decided I could give this primitive method a trial run, before reverting to the 'much better' Western model.

Nature had her way, and labour commenced, with a healthy baby being the outcome. Bunny-rugged baby daughter came home from the hospital after a few days, and a sleeping place on the marital bed was prepared. After getting over my initial fear of rolling right over my little daughter, I found it was a wonderful feeling to become involved with the nurturing process. The touch of a little hand holding my finger at 2am was good for her, and for me. This was true bonding taking place. Much better than standing over the cot and giving a goodnight kiss. Fathers did have a place, or a role, even at this early stage.

By the time Little Miss Marisa was six months old, I had to admit that my Western method had never given me the deep satisfaction that the Thai rearing was providing. This tiny being, of which I was part creator, was growing beside me. This can never equal the mother's feelings, where the child has grown inside her, but it's not a bad second best.

So I began to look at the previous Western ways to see if there were some good sociological reasons for the rabbits, ducks, swans and microphones. Yes, there was a benefit, I could immediately ascertain—for the retailers and manufacturers of said menagerie and electronic surveillance kits. But was there a benefit for the baby, or the parents?

After many years of medical practice, I have come to realise that we really are just animals, even though we pride ourselves on being top of the food chain, but still animals at heart. Human behaviour still reflects much of animal behaviour, and I have yet to hear of Mr and Mrs Lion placing the cubs in the cave next door every evening. No, the cubs stay with their mother and father, growing up safe and secure with their parents. That the human offspring should also be raised this way follows the same sociological and physiological pattern and should then be of no surprise.

Readers, I was wrong. We have outsmarted ourselves with our Western society. Put yourself in the position of the neonate. Which would you prefer—call out into the microphone above the cot, or place your little hand on a nice warm mother beside you for an immediate suckle? Rabbits, ducks, swans and microphones are a very poor substitute for living, breathing parents. And a loudspeaker in the master bedroom is an even poorer substitute for a living, breathing baby beside you.

I suggest it's no contest. Thailand wins.

~

Morning Walks

I AM WELL AWARE OF the fact that I should exercise more. So is my wife, who laboriously penned the message stuck on the door of my wardrobe stating: 'If you love me and your children, then exercise every morning.'

Medically I have to agree, but it is not that easy. To begin with, I am not a morning person. Mornings only have a six o'clock if you are coming home late. I do not function well in the mornings. Finding my mouth to insert the toothbrush requires a skill and dexterity that I do not possess at that time, even though I am theoretically awake. More than once, the toothbrush has found an errant nostril. Exercises as well? You have to be kidding.

Mind you, I did try. Honestly. Having made up my mind to at least try, I staggered into the bathroom and after finding my oral opening to insert the toothbrush, I tried running on the spot. Only to crash into the wall, because I forgot that the running was supposed to be on the same spot. The following morning I tried again. Making vigorous circles with my arms, I managed to break the towel rail. It was never going to work.

However, 'going to work' did become a (partial) answer to the exercise problem. The mighty Daihatsu Mira, my econo-car, let me down. A suspected blown head gasket necessitated my calling up Martin, my long-suffering garage owner, to tow the little white box away. Martin, I should add, is an enthusiast of large capacity V8 American iron, so I can imagine that he shudders every time he hears my voice, with yet another tale of woe regarding my 130,000 km, totally neglected daily mini-transport.

Martin rang me back with the usual combination of good and bad news that garage owners are so good at. The good news was that the car had been successfully towed to the workshop. The bad news was that it wasn't a cylinder head gasket, but that corrosion had eaten the cylinder head away, and a new cylinder head was going to be needed. The further bad news was the fact that there were no cylinder heads available, and he would have to try and find a reasonable second-hand one. I resigned myself to the fact that this was going to be no overnight job. This was going to take some time. It was also going to be necessary to get the wallet out.

Now, where I live is not far from Sukhumvit Road, that wonderful section of bitumen that runs from Bangkok to Cambodia, making it the longest road in the kingdom. The Daihatsu has not even warmed up by the time I have left my house and then turn left onto Sukhumvit, so it couldn't be far. It was then that I decided that I should walk to Sukhumvit and then catch the bus to work at the Bangkok Hospital Pattaya. After all, it couldn't be far.

The next morning, teeth cleaned and sparkling, I set off for Sukhumvit. I was muttering the mantra 'It can't be far,' over and over as I manfully set forth. I was so sure that it was not going to be far that I even turned down the offers of a lift from two passing taxi motorcycles. I smiled at the owners of little food stalls as they fired up the charcoal for that day, and wondered at the young women still in their pyjamas as they got their children ready and uniformed to be picked up by the school buses. I also saw, for the first time, that the vendors with barrows laden with cane furniture were part of a consortium. A truck was pulled over unloading several knocked down wheelbarrows which were being assembled to lug the furniture. So now I knew where they came from! For a while I honestly felt at one with nature.

About halfway to Sukhumvit, I began frequently changing the hand carrying my briefcase, this item being as usual ridiculously heavy, as for some reason I seem to be incapable of throwing papers away. And anyway, the weight does not matter when it is in the boot of a Daihatsu Mira! But it wasn't in the boot, was it?

Three quarters of the way up my street I was on snarling terms with a complete family of stray dogs. Thai dogs own the bitumen they sleep on and heaven help those who trespass. Such as I was doing. However, I also found that a briefcase can become a good weapon when swung with some accuracy.

I kept trudging, as the end was in sight. Well, Sukhumvit Road at least, and wearily I turned the corner to await the predatory *song taew* pickup buses, while fending off more taxi motorcycles.

At last, an empty one came along and with joy and relief I got out of the sun and into the taxi. However, the taxi driver was certainly not moving off for one solitary *farang*, and we waited for 10 minutes until the pickup was full of school children with bags, construction workers with tools and the odd office girl with containers of rice and a demented young chap holding wonderful conversations with himself. I suppressed the urge to write an immediate referral to Dr Somchai, the hospital psychiatrist. By now, we numbered 17, with 14 under cover and the remainder hanging off the back step. This was enough for the driver to fire up the diesel engine.

And so the ride to the hospital began, lurching and thumping over every pothole, as our *song taew* driver must have up-rated the springs to cater for its daily overloading. To add to the discomfort, every belching diesel truck seemed to be using the same stretch of road, and sand was whipping up from the six months of unfinished roadworks (after all, one should not rush into things as important as laying drains)!

After a spine-tingling 20 minutes I had arrived at the hospital, to find that the smallest denomination note in my possession was 100 baht. With an air of defeat

I pushed it through the passenger's window to the awaiting hand, expecting the usual claim of *'mai mee tang ton'* (no change), but was delighted to be happily given 90 baht in return! 10 baht for 20 minutes; at least there was value for money, even if I might have to spend it on X-Rays and painkillers.

But I digress. I did this form of morning exercise for two more days and then rang Martin to plead with him to finish the Mira. He responded and it was delivered that evening. The 1.1 km walks to Sukhumvit are over (I measured it later). I am now back to trying running on the spot, with a toothbrush in my mouth, and avoiding the new towel rail. However, mornings will never be quite the same again.

~

Thai Music; Music?

THERE WAS AN INTERESTING ITEM in *The Nation* newspaper the other day, detailing a group of musical artists of the '*mor lam sing*' (Thai/Isan) genre, who were heavily criticised for performing in the nude. *The Nation* was shocked, but for someone from the West, where we had nude singers in the hippy musical *Hair* 40 years ago, this was not so notable. *The Nation* did not publish photographs either. Spoil sports!

However, this item is not about public nudity, even if it did interest you enough to keep reading. It is about the amazing world of Thai music. If you go back far enough, Thai music came about several hundred years ago, and in typical Thai fashion, they invented their own musical scale. I am sure you were taught, like me, the 'solfa' scale of eight notes starting with Do, Re, Mi and so forth. Those who know, tell me that the eight notes are equidistantly spaced. You do not need rocket science to then see that any scale built on seven equidistantly spaced notes, such as the Thai one, will not coincide with the Western scale. Discord is the polite way to describe it.

Now, you also have to remember that Thai is a tonal language, where each word can have up to five meanings or even more, depending upon the tone spoken—high, medium, low, falling or rising. '*Mai*' can mean a question mark, no, new, wood, silk, microphone (a colloquialism) or burn. Well, this exceptional one has seven meanings. Still with me?

So if you want to say: 'New wood (or silk or microphone) doesn't burn, does it?' it could be written as '*mai mai mai mai mai*?' Perhaps you are now starting to understand why Thai is almost impossible for any *farang* over the age of 50 to learn, especially one who is becoming tone deaf.

However, I had always wondered just how a Thai singer did put the tones into the words in a song. If you gave a word a different tone, you would be changing the note which would then be theoretically singing off-key. Finally my query was answered by my friend, a radiologist, at morning tea. 'You cannot sing the tone, so you just guess the meaning,' he said. Mystery explained!

Fortunately, there would not be too many Thai songs with 'new wood doesn't burn, does it?' in the lyrics! No, Thai songs are all about love, rejection, the hardships of being away from home, boy yearns for girl, girl yearns for true love, and I just wish they would get together and stop singing.

Much of traditional Thai music is instrumental, but not using the kinds of instruments that you and I are conversant with, other than some strange indigenous drums and cymbals. At last count there were about 50 types of local versions of flutes, stringed instruments, and gongs used for all kinds of occasions: festivals, folk theatre, marriages, funerals, and social evenings after harvesting. And not to mention *Muay Thai* (Thai kickboxing) where it is used extensively in the interval between rounds. This music sounds very much like a cat being assaulted in a way that would bring the RSPCA out in force and criminal charges laid.

However, it should also be understood that as well as the traditional *'luk thung'*, *'mor lam'* and *'mor lam sing'*, there are many Western style bands and even Symphony Orchestras these days. The very revered King Of Thailand, His Majesty King Bhumibol Adulyadej the Great (Rama IX) is an internationally recognised jazz musician with numerous original compositions to his credit, one of which was featured in a Broadway show in the 1950s. He also appeared in *Time* magazine in 1960 with Benny Goodman, with the photo caption being 'The Kings of Swing'!

In 1964, the world renowned Institute of Music and Arts of the City of Vienna conferred its Honorary Membership upon His Majesty the King in recognition of his outstanding musical achievements. He became the 23rd Honorary Member of the Institute since its establishment in 1817, and the first Asian composer to receive this honour.

But we live these days in the shadow of MTV, and the pop music culture is everywhere, with the *'luk kreung'* (Eurasian) singers being the most popular, with names such as Tata Young and Bird Thongchai McIntyre showing the cultural mix.

However, there is another musical influence in Thailand that cannot be ignored: Karaoke. At the end of any Thai party, out comes the karaoke machine and some tipsy person grabs the microphone and begins to warble. This brings thunderous applause from everyone, followed by some misguided soul rushing up to the stage and presenting the singer with a rose. This is a mistake, as it only encourages both the singer to continue and the rest of the guests to become involved in rose showering. This is genuine cringe material.

Popular knowledge has it that karaoke started at a snack bar in Kobe City. It is said that when a guitarist could not come to perform at the bar due to illness, the owner of the bar prepared tapes of accompaniment recordings, and the customers enjoyed singing to the tapes. Even though its origins lie in legend, since then, karaoke has been commercialised and has become popular all over Japan, and then spread out across Asia before permeating the West. Better believe.

Chinese automobile maker, Geely Automobile, received much press in 2003 for being the first automaker to equip a car, their 'Beauty Leopard', with a karaoke machine as standard equipment. If it wasn't hard enough to drive in this traffic, you now have to contend with the driver charging down at you from your right, while loudly singing a Thai interpretation of Tina Turner, complete with leg kicks.

However, I have my own idea as to the origin of karaoke, and you can forget snack bars in Kobe City. Let them carry on growing Kobe beef. I believe karaoke is Japan's revenge for WW II. Think about it!

~

Different Places

AFTER BEING A DOCTOR FOR almost 40 years, and having experienced medicine in the UK, Europe, Australia and now Thailand, it never ceases to amaze me that there are so many similar, and yet vastly different ways that medicine is practised. It really is the often quoted 'Same, same but different' situation! (And yes, I know you've got the T-shirt!)

After qualifying in the UK several moons ago, followed by the necessary 'preregistration' year to teach the young graduate just how little he or she really knows, I found myself practising in Gibraltar. This was during yet another of their public referenda to see whether the population wanted to be British or Spanish. This was a no-brainer. Who wanted to be in a Spanish province when they could be 'British' and Mother England would pay the bills for them to be self-governing? 37 years ago, the rock was populated by

English speaking Barbary apes and Spaniards carrying Union Jacks.

I remember being asked to see the wife of the Minister of Tourism for Gibraltar, and being told, 'You spikkee Spanee. Me no spikkee Englee!' And yes, that year with a 99% positive turnout, Gibraltar remained British.

'Britee we are, Britee we stay,' was the successful slogan.

It was also in Gibraltar that I learned there were ethnic differences in the patients' expectations. I had noticed the Spaniards would bring with them a bottle of urine, irrespective of the medical problem. I asked my boss what I was supposed to do with the collection of bottles I would accumulate in the course of the day and it transpired that all I was supposed to do was hold them up to the light, mutter *orina bien* (urine's fine), look sage, and continue with the consultation. By this simple expedient, national customs were fulfilled and the patients left satisfied, leaving 'time' (the 'real healer') to happen naturally.

From there it was back to the UK and its much vaunted or despised NHS, depending upon which side of the fence you looked from. In those days, with no incentives for the government ruled doctors, and every incentive for the public to abuse the system (and the doctors), from my point of view it was a disaster. I would be dragged out of bed to attend to someone with blisters on their heels from wearing new shoes, or for a woman demanding cotton wool balls as she was stuffing cushions that evening. But they had all paid their National Health Service tax, so I had to do it!

I also experienced a bureaucracy that told me I could have no more blood for a patient, as he had already exceeded his quota! I replied by asking for the bureaucratic person's name, saying that I would personally wheel my patient down to his office so that I could show him the man who was going to let him die! Incidentally, I did get the blood. Or rather the patient did!

Fleeing to Australia was the answer, and I arrived at the great sunburned land of Down Under before the advent of the government's compulsory health insurance. This was a new experience for me. The patients paid after the consultation, or at the end of the month when the bill was sent. But perhaps never. One dozen fresh farm eggs were my payment from one poor family for 12 months of medical care. An egg a month, but it didn't really matter. What you lost on the swings, you got back on the roundabouts. It all seemed to work, but with the advent of a populist government, the universal Medicare insurance came in, something similar to Thailand's 30 baht scheme. But a lot more expensive, and more intrusive.

With the experience of the NHS in the UK behind me, I knew what would be next. The system was designed for abuse. With the patients freed from the shackles of payment, it opened the door of opportunity for the opportunists amongst the patients, and also amongst my colleagues. The profession became medical supermarketeers.

To survive I was going to have to adopt the 'Any fries to go with that?' mentality. I stumbled and fell at the cash register. This was not how I wanted to practice medicine.

So what could I do? I was by then 56 years old and enough was enough. Fleeing was again the only answer. It was then that I fled to Thailand. This move also meant that I was to give up active medical practice, as there is no reciprocity between Thailand and the UK, Europe or Australia, where I was fully registered as a doctor.

However, once a doctor, always a doctor, and when offered an advisory position with one of the local private hospitals I was flattered. They believed that a doctor of my years and experience would have knowledge that would be advantageous for them. I was staggered. Here was a country in which age and experience was a plus. Grey power actually working on a personal level. Walking through the hospital corridors and being deeply *wai*'d to by young doctors with Mayo Clinic qualifications is a wonderful boost to my older ego!

And so I began to lecture these young enthusiastic Thai doctors on the expectations of the foreign patients compared to the expectations of the Thai patients. And there are many differences. The locals feel cheated if they come away from the pharmacy without a large bag of multi-coloured pills, whilst the *farang*s would appear in my office asking, 'Which ones of these do I *have* to take?'

For me, Thailand has proved there is life after the Australian Medicare system. In the meantime I will ponder on all these bottles of urine that were left for me by a grateful Spanish visitor!

~

Weather, Global Warming and Y2K

EVERY TIME I GO TO the UK I marvel at the weather. I must say I marvel even more as to why anyone would (or could) put up with such weather and the change of seasons.

The UK claims it has a temperate climate (read any guidebooks), but my experience is that the seasonal temperate weather is Wet, Wet and Cold, Wet and Very Cold and finally Dry and Cold.

By comparison, the weather in Thailand also covers four seasons, but these are Hot, Hotter, Very Hot and Hot and Wet.

In fact, as I write this, the Old Bloke Upstairs, or God if you like, is hurling the water down in huge celestial bucket loads. It is difficult to imagine tropical downpours. You need to experience them.

In less than 15 minutes, the road is covered in so much water that the level flows over the pavements. In 30 minutes of deluge, the cars are sloshing through water up to axle height. After 60 minutes, large sections of highway have become lakes and small villages are cut off. But our rain is never cold. For the British reader, trying to imagine hot rain would be difficult, but believe me, it happens.

I think it is worth looking at global warming, too, if we are discussing the weather. In fact, the world conference on global warming took place in Bangkok in recent years, with the good news being that we have eight years to come up with the answer to this problem, which is threatening to change the planet into something like Mars.

The delegates stayed in the flash hotels, of which there are many in Bangkok, and ate caviar and drank champagne while pondering the problem. This was just getting themselves prepared for the privations that are coming, as the sun comes roaring through the hole in the ozone layer.

I hope they all managed to get home safely with their doggy bags. But how fortunate we are to have these selfless citizens who are going to lead us into the valley of temperate weather, while patching up the aforesaid hole.

Now I do not consider myself an expert in climate change. I am not even a climate watcher, though I will carry an umbrella in the wet season.

As an aside, have you ever stopped to wonder why it is that the rain always begins when you are in the office, but the umbrella is in the car? And the damn umbrella is always in the office, when it begins raining on the way home! I have tried to counteract this by having two umbrellas, but this always ends up within a week with two brollies in the car, and none in the office! Or vice versa. Perhaps the answer is three umbrellas.

But I digress. I did also mention Y2K, the Millennium Bug that was going to bring the world to its knees as the clock struck 12 on the eve of 31 December 1999. Planes were going to crash, banks would erupt, ATMs would explode, and we would all be ruined.

Fortunately, a group of white knights appeared and (for a certain sum of money), these clever IT chappies would check your computer and make it safe. You even got a sticker proclaiming your equipment was Y2K safe! Bug free and bug resistant.

However, there were some that did not heed the doomsayers. And I was one of them. I did not call up the cavalry, but by using simple logic, I went into that dark area of the computer which governs the date and time, and set the internal clock for 11.59pm on 31 December 1999.

I had less than one minute to wait to see if my computer would turn into a flaming mass of semiconductors as the clock ticked into the new millennium. We—my computer and I—entered into my 'virtual' 2000 without even the slightest cough or hiccup. The Millennium Bug was mysteriously absent. Put the aerosol can of pesticide away. Totally not required.

No, I believe that the Millennium Bug was something a section of the world's community managed to dream up. Likewise, the global warning soothsayers, have more to gain from the situation than the planet does.

But then, I always was a cynic. I cannot help thinking back to my history lessons at school. Where did the Ice Age come from? The ozone layer quadrupled itself or what? What climate change fried the dinosaurs? And fry, they certainly did.

How else do you explain dinosaur footprints in mud? Try leaving your own footprints in mud for posterity and tell me if they are still there after the next rainy day. You have to fire the clay, as any basic village potter in Northeast Thailand will tell you, who has managed to live through Y2K (and the recent coup) unscathed.

So did the ozone layer fall down from its sky hooks? I dunno, but there is an army of world experts out there willing to eat caviar and drink champagne while staying in flash hotels at my expense, and telling me how to avert tragedy. (More caviar and champagne it seems is on the agenda.)

No, I think I will take my chances out here in Thailand. My car is air-conditioned. My house and office ditto. The roof in the new house doesn't leak and my umbrella's in the car.

What more do I need? (More umbrellas?) And I know the Hot and Wet season will follow the Very Hot season, as it has always done since the days of the first settlers in Thailand. All is well with the world.

Now I must go and dry my shoes.

~

Living Through Drought

MY DEAR OLD DAD WAS a connoisseur of single malt whiskeys. As a lad I was taught that the only liquid that goes with a good Scotch was pure water. In fact, the very name 'whiskey' comes from the Gaelic, or Irish, *'uisce beatha'* and means the 'water of life'. Unfortunately Dad was wrong. Living in Thailand has taught me that the water of life is a two litre bottle of Evian.

I only happened across this essential reality when Jomtien, where I live, found itself waterless recently. Noticing a burst water main one evening did not really prepare me for the next day. After all, I was used to water being free and plentiful. Water was for diluting alcohol and not for worshipping or even speaking about in reverent tones!

The next morning I went for my usual Australian dingo's breakfast (a pee and a walk around) and noticed the loo wouldn't flush. Turned on the tap—nothing! Disaster!

Gathering a towel around me I rushed out into the street to see if someone had stolen my meter or turned the supply cock off. No, everything was fine. Fine, other than the fact that I had no water.

I am not a morning person and cannot function without a shower as my wake-up, so I began looking for water anywhere in the house.

Never mind, there was a 2 litre bottle of Evian in the kitchen. Unfortunately, in the refrigerator in the kitchen. With water, albeit cold, I returned to the bathroom. Now, necessity is the mother of invention, they say, so there I was, cloth in one hand and cold Evian in the other, having the worst possible birdbath in the world while shiveringly collecting my thoughts. But at least I now had a plan!

The first item was to see if this water shortage was a local phenomenon or general. My local laundry across the street looked a good bet so I enquired there. *'Mai nam mai?'* (For those with even less Thai than I, this is roughly translated as 'No water?')

She nodded, and said there would be none for three days! She then indicated to follow her to the rear of the shop. There were lots of large containers with water in them. Light was beginning to dawn ... Those large plastic bins the previous owner had left, which were now happily being used as rubbish containers, were not for rubbish at all, were they! They were for water!

She then turned to me and said, 'You not got bum?' Now, whilst her English is not good, it is definitely better than my Thai, but references to my anatomy seemed out of place here. I looked perplexed.

'Bum for water,' she continued ... 'Oh, pump,' I replied, relieved that we could continue our commercial laundry arrangements without awkwardness.

There was a small room at the back of my house with an evil looking well in it—that *must be the pump room*, I thought. Thanking Madam Laundry I rushed home again.

Indeed, there was a pump with a pipe heading skywards. Outside the house I could then spot the tank on the roof. I burst into laughter—the cavalry had come.

The second part of the plan was to get local reinforcements, so I dressed and waited for the maid. After she arrived I pantomimed the problem (Marcel Marceau has nothing on me, I tell you), and prepared for action. I turned valves in different directions and with the maid now poised beside the pump switch I climbed on to the roof.

'Turn on bum,' I yelled and almost immediately water began to course into the tank, only to stop almost as quickly. 'On bum, on bum,' I yelled again.

'*Mee pun ha,*' (There's a problem) was the reply. It was only then, after the high of elation had dissolved, that I realised I was being bitten by hundreds of small creatures. I now had a pressing problem of my own—ants—to add to water shortages.

Back on the ground and now covered in Baygon and calomine I reviewed the situation. I did have a 'bum' but it wouldn't work and I had several water containers which were all full of rubbish. Mind you, I still had half a bottle of Evian.

Resisting the desire to drink it with a bottle of single malt there and then, I took the housemaid in the car and we went water hunting. Eventually we ran down a water truck who came to the house and filled all our containers, after we emptied the rubbish out, plus any large pots and pans. And all for 50 baht. I gave him 60, I was so relieved!

Fortunately, the mains water supply was repaired within one day so I have running loos and hot showers again. And I am just so much more savvy about living in Thailand—but can somebody please tell me how I keep all these large containers of water algae free till next time?

~

Songkran

LIKE MOST FARANGS I TRY to leave Thailand during the Thai New Year, that time of fun, sun and 'sanook' (fun, amusement), called Songkran.

There are several good reasons for this and I will let you in on some of them; reasons which have been made abundantly clear to any ex-pat who has lived here for any length of time.

The first concept to master is that the Thais do not 'celebrate' their New Year, such as we do, (and Thais celebrate our New Year too), but they will say they are going to 'play' Songkran. The first difference should now be apparent.

In 'playing' Songkran, the idea is to pour water on every other person, and be similarly doused yourself. This is done with great hilarity and amusement, and is (in theory) the way Thais get through the hottest time of the year, in April. A cooling bath sounds very practical. But forget about Thai pragmatism and anything else you have read. This is how the Thais have taken one of the nicest ceremonies and debased it, unfortunately aided and abetted by the foreigners. Us.

Songkran is actually a Sanskrit word in Thai form which means the entry of the sun into any sign of the Zodiac, but the *Songkran* in this particular instance is when the sun enters the sign of Aries or the Ram. Its full name is *Maha Songkran* or 'Major' *Songkran* to distinguish it from the other ones. *Songkran* is in fact the celebration of the vernal equinox similar to those of the Indian *Holi* Festival, the Chinese *Ching Ming*, and the Christian festival of Easter.

Originally, *Songkran* was the time when families traditionally got together. The younger members of the family would venerate their elders and show respect by gently pouring lustral water over the hands and feet of their older relatives, and ask forgiveness for past misdeeds. Buddha images were also similarly treated. It was a time of circumspectness and renewing family ties.

However, Thais are a fun-loving (*sanook*) people and it became the norm that the younger members would also have water sprinkled at them. This would bring good luck, another much desired feature in Thai life.

Over the years, this gradually degenerated into an all-out water fight after the elders had their hands in the water, and the modern form of *Songkran* was beginning to unfold.

Now you have to remember that this is still Thai New Year, so it is a public holiday (13-15 April are the official days). Again, this was such that the younger members could travel to the family village, venerate the elders, meet up with each other and wish all family members the best for the forthcoming year, and then return to the province where they were now working.

Taking this to the extreme, this meant one day for travelling, one day for the elders, one day for a water fight and one day to return. *Songkran* became a four-day event.

Now, since the water fight was so much fun, why restrict water fights to just one day? Why indeed. *Songkran* became four days of water dousing. News of a four day, fun-filled water fight soon trickled back to the West and those who enjoyed the odd recreational stoush or benevolent brawl began coming over to 'play' *Songkran* as well, leaving behind their football club scarves, as it is generally around 40 degrees Celsius at this time in Thailand.

The foreign invasion also brought some technology with it (as well as the aggression that *farang*s are so adept at), to add to the fun aspect of *Songkran;* the water pistol. Not the little hand-held item you used as a child, but something more akin to a bazooka. In fact I have actually seen a firefighter's water cannon mounted in a pickup. You could now have a backpack with several gallons of water. Mayhem (or aquatic Armageddon) was coming!

However, sheer volume of water was not enough. The professional *Songkran* player needed to add some more dimensions. The first was talcum powder, to liberally daub the wetted victim, but this soon changed to 'prickly heat' powder, which has a stinging ingredient to really let the victim know that he or she has been marked. It also allows some not too subtle fondling of the female form during the application.

The next step up was to, rather than just throw or squirt ambient-temperature water at everyone, realise that iced water would have a much greater effect at producing a response. The backpack was filled with ice cold water! The school bullies were now in their element. Domination, power and pain at their disposal.

Unfortunately there is yet another aspect to celebrating (or playing) Thai New Year. Just like the Western world's New Year, or the Scottish Hogmanay, it is considered de rigueur that one gets totally blotto to celebrate the coming of another year. Why, I do not know, but I am as guilty as the rest of you, for that one night. But over here, the Thais spend four days drinking Thai whiskey, which is guaranteed to give anyone a splitting headache and the tremors by day three. If you live that long.

There is now another item to be factored in. The never-ending love affair with the motorcycle. All Thai families have at least one, and generally one per person. Now try riding down the street, several sheets to the wind, and being hit in the face with iced water at Force 10. Correct! You fall off. However, since the vast majority of Thais do not wear a crash helmet, you land on the road head first at 30 km/h. If you think that doesn't really hurt, then try jumping out of a car head first at even 20 km/h, and get your relatives to tell me how you got on.

But there is a serious note here. The awful statistics, as I wrote this item, indicated that this year over 100 people were killed and several hundred injured—and that was by day two of the festival. There was more to come folks, many more. In fact the usual number of fatalities over *Songkra*n is around 600, with several thousand merely injured. And 85% of the fatalities come from motorcycle riders. Am I the only one to see the connection?

So we have a water bath which has become a blood bath, now spread over around one week, as four days was not enough time to really have some fun playing *Songkran*. This sort of 'fun' I can do without.

For those of us who could not get away for some reason or other, it is a time of barricading oneself in, and making sure the car doors are locked while driving (yes, they will wrench the door open and give you a fun-filled bucket of iced water as you drive to work in your good clothes).

But on one afternoon, I will go down to the road from our village with the children, and throw water over those who stop beside us, who do the same to us in return. This is done with gentleness and friendliness and good humour. It is as close to the spirit of the old *Songkran* that I can get.

That is, if I cannot get away.

~

The *Songkran* water festival; a celebration of the vernal equinox
that has mutated into a four-day, all-out water fight, can lead to
the slowest, and wettest traffic jams you could ever see. Whole
families armed with hoses and water cannons throng the streets.

Life in the Slow and Wet Lane

IT IS DIFFICULT TO DESCRIBE what it is like 'playing' *Songkran*, but have you ever been involved in a traffic jam? A traffic jam so bad that you could not even imagine it in your wildest dreams? During this time, it is not just the slow progress of the traffic—it took me three hours to cover three kilometres—but the attendant large-scale lunacy.

This was not the psychiatric condition known as *'folie a deux'* where one person talks another into having the first person's delusions; *Songkran* is *'folie a tout le monde'* where everybody goes mad!

This year, I took the extended family (wife and children plus nanny, maid and a cousin) into Pattaya to have a look at the festivities first-hand.

This was an irrevocable and masochistic decision, as once you begin to funnel into the event, there is no way out.

The realisation that you are caught in a *Songkran* traffic jam is very close to claustrophobia. There really is no way out. You are caught in it, and then caught up with it.

Imagine you are stopped behind a pickup truck. In the bed of the pickup is at least one central 44 gallon drum of water, surrounded by up to a dozen young Thais of all ages and sexes (remembering that we have three official sex designations in Thailand—men, women, and women of the second category), each with a small bucket containing water, or a mix of water and talcum powder. And everyone on board is dripping wet.

To the right of you is another pickup, similarly 'armed'. There is another, right behind you, heading up a line as far as you can see. Coming towards you is another long line-up of pickups, doing the one kilometre per hour claustrophobic crawl as well.

That is not all. Between the pickups are endless motorcycles weaving through impossibly small spaces, carrying anything between one and four people, all wet, all carrying water weapons of various sizes, from small hand-held items to larger ones complete with water backpacks.

But there is yet more. Lining the pavements are groups of revellers with their own water drums, garden hoses and talcum powder. This group of drowned rats rushes out between the lines of cars, motorcycles and pickups, stopping any forward movement of the traffic, to throw more water at close range, or smear the talcum powder on the faces of the young pretty girls on motorcycles.

Everyone in this *Songkran* celebration is soaked. Everyone is dancing to incessant music pumped out of enormous loudspeakers. Everyone is throwing water. Everyone is being daubed with talcum powder mixture. Everywhere is madness.

Those sightseers like us, cocooned in our firmly locked car, are asked, in mime, to wind the windows down just a little, to have a respectful daub of talcum. The unsuspecting do so and are immediately drenched. We are old hands and do not.

However, in retaliation for non-compliance, our windscreen is heavily smeared with talcum mixture and the windscreen wipers pulled off the screen so we cannot wipe it clean. We are blind, but the next deluge of water soon washes it away and we can see again.

There was another development this year—rubber masks, with everything from Osama bin Laden through to Batman, just in case the scene wasn't surreal enough. These masked marauders would also parade through the traffic, complete with water containers and talcum. Nobody is spared. Every prisoner is taken.

However, there is another dimension to these Thai New Years; food. Thais cannot go long without eating, and walking through the mayhem are people selling bags of hard-boiled eggs, to be greedily gobbled, washed down with the endless bottles of beer, either bought at the side of the road, or kept in the back of the pickups, between the water drums.

But there is more than just the hard-boiled eggs. In between boom boxes on the pavement are the mobile kitchens selling polystyrene boxes of noodles. (The fare might be primitive, but Thailand has embraced the modern polystyrene culture with both hands. In 50 years time, you will still be able to see what we ate in 2007!) But getting back to *Songkran*; everyone may be wet and talcum powdered, but at least they are not hungry.

Songkran is a life experience that everyone who comes to Thailand should experience once. On that first time, incredulity gives way to abandonment and enjoyment. The second time, the experience is less enjoyable. If there is a third time, you should see someone about your innate masochism.

You have until April next year to either find the cure, or book your seat out of the place. But don't go to Laos, Cambodia or Burma. They have their own water throwing festivals as well. Take my tip: Stay dry!

~

You Know You are Better When You Can Pass Wind

ONE FACT WHICH IS NOT taught at medical school is that doctors are not allowed to fall sick. I have examined the Hippocratic Oath carefully, and nowhere does it say that by becoming a doctor you have now been given a special card providing an instant immunity to all diseases. However, cough twice and you are immediately regaled with, 'Doctors aren't supposed to get sick.' Or, 'Can't you cure yourself, Doc?' Physician heal thyself indeed. Let me assure you that doctors are merely human, and subject to all the normal human frailties. Not that I like admitting to it!

So, on to this little piece. I was going to head this item: 'You know you're better when you can fart,' but knowing that the editor might feel this was in bad taste, I didn't. Even though this is usually thought of as more malodorous than the other! I could even have called it, 'The oyster and my porcelain friend.' The world is your oyster they say, but for me it was the reverse—the damned oyster took over my world.

What happened was that my wife brought home a bag of fresh oysters from the local market. It was no special champagne celebration, or scientific test in the making to see if they all worked, but merely a bargain spotted and capitalised upon. They were lovely, eaten that evening with some fried garlic and a very small dob of chilli sauce. Without a drop of alcohol passing my lips (true!), I retired to bed at 11pm to wake very suddenly at midnight with my mouth awash, a tingling feeling in my cheeks and the awful realisation that I was going to vomit.

With an agility that would have made an Olympic Triple Jumper envious, I hopped smartly out of bed, stepped on the cat, and jumped into the toilet, emptying the contents of my stomach into the porcelain bowl with a technicolour yawn. As an aside, have you ever wondered why, when you vomit, it is always diced carrot? Even if you haven't eaten a carrot for weeks! Another medical mystery.

I returned to bed, to repeat the Olympic performance 20 minutes later, but by now it was bright yellow acrid bile I was offering up as I knelt at the altar of the porcelain gods. And again 20 minutes after that, and on and on and on, with more encores than Mick Jagger and Nellie Melba combined.

By four in the morning, the Olympic athlete was dragging a battered belly from bed to toilet and back. It was time to forget about pride and my boast of being 'always well'. I was put in the car, clutching a large bowl, and my wife drove me to the Bangkok Hospital Pattaya, where I work.

It did not need bringing in a brain surgeon to the casualty department to work out that I had a case of acute food poisoning, and one of those oysters would have been the culprit. I already knew the diagnosis, but having agreed upon it with the examining doctor, the next move was treatment, and that is fluid replacement.

The intravenous drip was soon in place, and some anti-vomiting medication and anti-spasmodic drugs were sent up my IV line, where my body was waiting. In a daze I was transferred to a private room, where the angels in white were waiting to tuck me in. There was also the usual bed in the room for relatives of the patient, a concept that is not universal all over the world, but one that I do strongly believe in. There is nothing more comforting than to know one's partner is there, caring and watching over you. Anything to allay anxiety is good for the speedy recovery of any patient. And it makes it easier to go to the loo without strangers being present.

By the next morning, Mr Oyster's toxins had reached my lower bowel, and their departure from my gastro-intestinal tract was aided by rapid peristalsis and loud noises. This is medical jargon for 'the runs' and other euphemisms for diarrhoea ('diarrhea' if you 'voted' for George Bush).

Now there are a couple of schools of medical thought here. The one I adhere to does not include something to immediately stopper you up, like Imodium. The body (in this case the bowel) knows what is best and is rapidly excreting the problem. What is important now is electrolyte replacement therapy (the crystals you dissolve in water) to stop the body becoming unbalanced in its electrolytic make-up. What is not known to many, is that the bowel is really a giant water absorber to keep everything in balance. That's why 'normal' faeces is semi-solid.

'Ah, I see,' I can hear you muttering, as you contemplate a change of career to medicine, if it's that simple.

After a few hours I had improved enough to be disconnected from my lifeline, (alright, intravenous line to be more correct), but after a good attack of gastroenteritis you are as weak as a one-day-old puppy. I exchanged my hospital bed for my one at home, and continued to rest for the next few hours.

And as I said at the start of this item—you know you're better when you can fart! Sitting here now, I can safely say that I'm better!

~

Do as You are Told

I WAS BROUGHT UP BY my parents to be obedient. Extreme retribution could follow transgression of the edicts, so I have maintained that *raison d'être* to this day. However, sometimes I think the retribution might be better than following the commandments.

Take, if you will, some of these recent examples that I have been confronted with, from an uncaring and unfeeling hierarchy.

In a fit of whimsy, one of my newspaper clients decided I should travel on one of the cheaper carriers to Chiang Mai. I did everything that was needed of me—queued for an eternity in the Don Muang departure lounge to finally get to the smiling young man who gave me my seat allocation after I asked for an aisle seat as far forward in the plane as possible (if you are going to crash, get it over with quickly is my motto). Now with seat stub number 26 A (26 rows back and next to the window, thank you smiling young man) I walked the several kilometres to gateway 164 (well at least it seemed like gateway 164 it was so far away), going through the ignominy of having some young lady rubbing an electric mini cricket bat over me, while feeling my wallet to estimate my financial worth and whether I was carrying a spare roll of film in my pocket.

After all this I was rushing, because by now it was past the time indicated for boarding, to find that the plane had not even arrived at Don Muang to carry me to the Rose of the North, let alone being ready for take-off. I did however get to talk to the next pilot who was waiting there too, a lovely chap, comfortingly in his 50s who assured me that he had spent 20 years in the air force before going 'commercial' ten years ago. Not being a lover of plane travel, it is reassuring to find that the man at the sharp end has been there, done that, and isn't looking to star with Tom Cruise in a sequel movie to *Top Gun*.

When the incumbent pilot deigned to bring a plane for my ex-USAF *Top Gun* jockey to fly, we were eventually herded aboard, after that small army of cleaners had finished collecting toffee wrappers, discarded packets of peanuts, sick bags and the other detritus of the jet-setting traveller, from the inbound leg.

Not wishing to hold him up, as we were already 30 minutes late, I found my seat and sat down quickly. Then came the first of the commandments: 'Fasten seat belt while seated.' So said the sign on the back of the seat in front of me. But by now I was in a rebellious mood and ignoring my parental 'tapes', I tried to do it standing up, but I found I kept hitting my head on the overhead storage locker, and the belts weren't long enough to reach around me while vertical. So this was most sage advice, even if a trifle obvious. (My advanced years have also taught me that there are many things that are difficult to do standing up, but I will not elaborate, this being a family publication, if you get my drift.)

The next commandment was directly under the first, and at eye height for a child of three, but by peering down I was able to make it out quite plainly: 'Live vest under your seat,' said the sign—this was definitely more worrisome. How big was this 'live' vest? Why were we carrying livestock? Yes, livestock, as by squirming around in the seat I could see that my fellow impecunious passengers were also carrying a 'live vest' under their nether regions. I began waiting for someone in the crew to stand up and begin the safety announcements with, 'My fellow passengers, including the live vests, we are now headed for Chiang Mai …'

I started to apply some logical thought to this conundrum. What were these live vests doing? Had they paid for tickets too? Was this how the airline managed to keep the price down? Two live items carried per seat. One human on top and a vest underneath? Cunning devils!

However, fears for my own safety began to take over, as always happens when my feet are no longer in contact with terra firma. Was this live creature going to reach up and grab me by the cojones, halfway through my packet of peanuts, just when I was least expecting it?

Worse still, was there some kind of person wearing this live vest? Something like that dreadful crouching, leaping creature spouting gibberish in the *Lord of the Rings*? Fortunately, the flight was only one hour, so I was able to escape the vest's clutches whilst it must have remained asleep.

Let me finish with a third commandment I saw elsewhere: 'Turn engine off while parking.' This order was in the car parks of one very large, internationally renowned hotel in Pattaya. However, while trying to follow the directions, I found that with today's vehicles, when the engine is turned off, the power steering does not work, and the ignition key locks the steering wheel. By the time I had actually parked the car, pushing it into the parking space provided, I was too hot and sweaty for the meeting I had come for, so left my apologies and went home for a shower.

You have all been warned! Sometimes it is better not to follow commandments.

~

The Lucky Scorpion

MY FIRST KITCHEN COLUMN SAW me recounting the dramas of my wife finding a cobra in the kitchen. It was standing up to greet her, caul unfurled and fangs ready, when she opened the cupboard under the sink. Since then, she has perhaps been a little more circumspect before flinging open the cupboards.

However, the other evening, I was tapping away at the keyboard when suddenly a scream emanated from the kitchen. Like all good husbands, I breathed through my nose, saved the document I was working on, and strolled into the kitchen. The terrified one was pointing to the floor whilst staying in a somewhat rigid, if not quite catatonic pose.

Following the outstretched finger revealed a shiny black scorpion on the tiled floor. Two brawny arms at the front, armed with a set of claws that any self-respecting crab would have been proud of, and its tail arched over its back, in a 'come and get me if you dare' pose.

Quickly I assessed the situation and, grabbing an aluminium colander close to the sink, turned it upside down and dropped it neatly over our friend the scorpion. My wife then ran away, saying, 'Don't kill it. That would be bad luck.'

As an aside, I mentally wondered about all the bad luck that countless generations of Isan go-go dancers must have endured, eating these things deep-fried on a nightly basis, but I returned to the office, grabbed a substantial magazine and returned to the kitchen. With great skill and daring, I slid the magazine under the colander, neatly trapping the scorpion. Opening the kitchen window I prepared to introduce the black insect to the wonderful world of nocturnal high jumping.

Carefully I turned the colander the right way up and slid the magazine back, to reveal—an empty colander. In the words of the great comedians, 'There he was! Gone!' I felt like David Copperfield having performed another impossible illusion, except there was no audience, as well as no scorpion. And I am not David Copperfield.

My next panicky seconds were taken up with ensuring that I was not wearing the pesky varmint, and then I got down to floor level to see if he was there somewhere, and sure enough, he was. Stretched out and hugging the floor near the far wall, even his tail down, he presented a slim, sleek outline, and with his powerful pincers had obviously lifted the rim of the light colander enough for him to make good his escape.

Not to be outwitted by a scorpion, I selected a large, heavy based pot, within which I would trap him. With eyes watching each other's every move, I came closer. He took up battle stations again, claws at the ready, and sting at the even readier. But I was too quick for him, and neatly dropped the up-ended pot on top of him, in a clever flanking movement with my right arm, while fixing his gaze straight ahead. Round 2 to the human.

Even more carefully, I placed the magazine on the floor and dragged the pot over it, carefully checking that there was no scorpion anatomy sticking out from the rim of the pot. Once again, I lifted the pot and magazine, neatly turned it over and slid the magazine slowly back. This time David Copperfield failed, and there, running around the base of the pot, was my scorpion.

After reassuring it that it was not going to be Number 88's from the nearest chrome pole palace and dancing academy's dinner, it settled, and I took him outside and gave him an instant lesson in pole vaulting. Well, landings anyway. He slithered away into the undergrowth, and I am hopeful that he has appreciated the chance he was given in attempting immortality. Well, for a short time at least.

My wife was also very appreciative of my efforts, and declared that this would bring good luck. So much so, that she got up early the next morning to seek out the local lottery ticket seller, that being the last day, apparently, to do so. It certainly sounded as if releasing scorpions to the wild had much more cachet than (re)releasing the small caged birds proffered to every *farang* at the local *wat*.

It would be nice to report that after this episode, the lottery ticket returned the hoped-for six million baht, but no such luck, I am afraid. My then 18-month-old daughter removed said lottery ticket from her mother's handbag and has hidden it somewhere that would be suitable for the crown jewels. She has several repositories like these at this stage, and each is seemingly more secure than the last one. I firmly expect to find my bedside clock sometime this century, for example. Although probably not until after the batteries have turned into corrosive gel.

We have also had a minor accident with the car, which cost 7,000 baht to repair, but I suppose we can deduct that from the six million, after we find the ticket. To compound the 'luck', I have been diagnosed with a chronic kidney ailment that will necessitate my taking expensive drugs for the rest of my life. I'll deduct that expense from the six million too, but I have the sneaking suspicion that even if we do find we had the winning ticket, six million will probably be almost enough to fill the tank on the repaired family chariot.

In retrospect, I think I should have just banged the black beast on the head, despite my wife's entreaties, and made a donation to Number 88 at the go-go bar in case she felt hungry. At least somebody would have got some good luck out of the episode. So far, it certainly hasn't been me.

~

Above and Right: Making merit at temples and shrines such as these is an important part of life all over Thailand, both spiritually and culturally. With typical Thai pragmatism, you can have your fortune read with a *suemsee,* but if you don't like what you have been told, you can always pay for another.

A Coffin, Purgatory, and a Long Life

ONE DAY I PURCHASED A coffin for a poor person, saved my parents from purgatory, secured a long life for myself, and kept my wife happy. That's not bad for 30 minutes and £3.50 (or AUS$8.50)!

I have mentioned before that Thai people are superstitious. No, make that 'very' superstitious! My wife is Thai and all of the above applies. In spades.

But back to the story. I was rung breathlessly at lunchtime, just after I had paid for the coffin of a deceased man who had been poor in life, and had become no richer upon dying.

'Are you beezy?'

'No. Not too busy,' I replied guardedly.

'Then please meet me at the Sawang Boriboon Foundation as it is important for you to make merit.'

Now the Sawang Boriboon Foundation is a Chinese-based group that comes under the general heading of 'The Body Snatchers'! Thais are somewhat afraid of violent deaths, so the Chinese chaps clean up the road carnage.

It is a quick ride to the local *wat*'s crematorium office. However, if you are only severely injured rather than killed outright, you will be taken at high speed in the back of a pickup truck to the closest hospital. If you survive the trip, then you'll probably live through it all, though sometimes I think it might be better to just croak at the roadside. It would be quicker and less painful.

The Sawang Boriboon Foundation is also a charity organisation, and as I drove there that rainy Monday, I had the feeling that my wallet was about to become a sacrifice to somebody's gods somewhere.

However, as I arrived, the bright smile on the face of my wife was enough to make me happy too. I was informed that she had been to see the fortune teller that morning, and he had told her she was married to an older *farang* (true) and that I had just had a birthday (also true) but for everything to work out well for 2007, I had to make merit. The stage was set.

We went to the Sawang Boriboon merit counter, something similar to a teller's window at the bank, where I gave the smiling lady 250 baht, and in return she gave me a piece of yellow paper to fill out with the date and my name. This was signed by her and returned to me. A sort of receipt that I would be able to show later at the Merit Bank, I presumed. But it wasn't that easy. I was also given a piece of white paper headed 'Prayers for Benefactors'.

The instructions were quite plain. 'Walk upstairs. Light three joss sticks. Put the palms together and pray to the gods on the altar.'

There was much more about prayers and incantations, and at the bottom was the rider, 'You'd better buy a bottle of oil for worship and add oil to the lamp. God will bless you.'

Just coincidentally I am sure, there was a booth selling small bottles of cooking oil and packets of joss sticks that one passed on the way to the stairs, so for another 50 baht or so, we were oiled and jossed and ready.

We ascended the stairs, and on the next floor up there were several statues of Chinese gods, receptacles for incense and 'eternal' flames (re)fuelled by small bottles of recently purchased cooking oil. I also noticed that there were several large empty oil tins behind, one with 'The Pizza Company' label on it. I wondered idly if they were collecting or donating!

However, I did as I was instructed and poured my oil in as well and lit my three joss sticks and read aloud the prayers. These included my telling the altar gods that I had just donated a coffin to someone departed who had no relatives, and that I wanted the merits from my donation to reach my parents, (with the celestial instructions prompting me to say their names out loud). Since my father died 30 years ago, I hoped the message was not too late, but as my dear mother was still alive, this would be some handy insurance!

The instructions now read, 'When the praying is finished, please burn the yellow piece of paper called *anumotana* (or -*dana* which means *'rejoicing in the merit of the donor'*). I was a little disappointed at this, as I was sure I was supposed to have this with me, along with my lunchbox, when I arrived at the pearly gates. However, I burned the evidence of my philanthropy as directed.

But it was not over yet. My wife took me to another statue with an even bigger altar and pressed 17 lit joss sticks between the supplicant palms. 'Ask for a long life,' was whispered in my ear, so I duly put in the request and then split my joss sticks between the five awaiting urns.

Returning to the prayer space in front of the altar, I was given a large bamboo container with prayer sticks in it called *suemsee*. I had seen this done before, where you shake the bamboo and rattle the sticks until one pops out. It will have a number and you then take the same numbered fortune slip from the wall, and the future is revealed. Number 11 came out and immediately pulled from the nail. It had the future in Thai, Chinese and English and included the statement: 'Existing mate is a good match.' My wife, who was reading it over my shoulder, looked pleased.

I asked if anyone ever gets a bad reading, and was assured that this did happen, but it was not all downhill from there. In typical Thai fashion, there was a 'get-out' clause, my wife told me.

'If you don't like the ticket, then you burn it and get some more joss sticks and get another number from the shaker!'

With a slight drizzle still coming down, I was then led to the final altar, where I made more wishes, holding another three joss sticks, and with my eyes screwed tightly shut. As the thought, *I hope all this is worthwhile* irreverently came into my mind, a large drop of rain landed on my head, just to remind me where I was! I might have professed to being a card-carrying atheist for the past 40 odd years, but that didn't give me the right to think those kinds of thoughts in such celestial circumstances.

So merit was made, a coffin was bought, parents were taken from the fires of hell and my wife was happy that she was apparently assured of a 'good match' husband for some time yet. Where else in the world could you get such a lunchtime bargain? Only in Thailand.

PS. I was informed later that the fortune teller has predicted I will live to be 104, provided I remember to make merit each birthday. I think I might just skip a few towards the end. 100 will be enough for me!

~

Dining Out On Trees and Weeds

My very good friend, who introduced me to Thailand 30-odd years ago and who enjoyed the Kingdom so very much, was however, very afraid of the food. His staple diet was bananas. Unpeeled, so that nobody could touch the edible part!

Elsewhere in this book, I have written about my first meal in Thailand, and its effect on my mouth, throat, oesophagus (gullet), and the after effects the next day. This was enough to scare me off Thai food for a while too, but when you live here, there is a limit to how often you are prepared to dine out at a European restaurant for the compulsory steak and two veg.

When you start to talk about dietary items, it is often said by those who should know better, that 'You are what you eat.' This is of course, total nonsense. Do vegetarians turn into carrots? Does a weekend BBQ turn you into a ground-pawing steer? Obviously not. You are a living, breathing human being. End of story.

However, the shape you present to the outside world does depend upon what you eat.

By the way, there is probably more rubbish written about diets, diet foods and dieting than any other subject in the world. Every third person you meet is either on a diet, just got off a diet or about to go on a diet (after the New Year, her son's Bar Mitzvah or the swearing in of the next US president).

Diets run the whole gamut of extremes from the Israeli Army diet where you eat nothing but bananas and sand, to others put forward by multi-level marketers where you make up and drink three sachets of expensive powdered goop every day that will get the weight off you in one week. Or others where you eat their specially modified 'diet' foods. Funny that, when they aren't adding anything to the food, they are actually leaving sugar and other expensive nasties out! Trust me! I am a doctor!

So where does all this gluttony come into living in Thailand? Well everything you read above relates to living in the West, where we all came from. I can remember eating bread and dripping as a child: 100% cholesterol on a carbohydrate base. It's a wonder we all managed to live past 30. Mind you, some of us didn't, but those of us who are still going are paying for it now, with coronary artery bypass surgery and drug eluting stents and other such expensive ways to get the clag out of our coronary arteries.

Now, the Thai population never used to have such coronary artery problems, because they had a diet which was not high in animal fats. Cows are as rare as honest politicians in Thailand. Milk and cheese are almost unheard of. And as for steaks? Who was going to kill a perfectly good steer (or even buffalo) that can still bring in money? Sick buffaloes are an industry leader all on their own. Ask any lady from the bar.

No, the Thai diet was mainly rice and vegetables, foodstuffs which will not put the weight on. Mind you, some of the vegetables are a little suspect. For example, my wife will be driving along the road, and will screech to a halt and leap out to come back with some weed or other, which I am assured is totally edible. Perhaps in its natural state, but covered with industrial fallout and car exhausts I have to wonder.

But back to the basic, original Thai vegetable and rice based diet—this low calorie diet explains why many years ago, the Thai ladies were all slim little poppets, with breast development in the two fried eggs category. However, all that has changed.

There are now Thai ladies with Pamela Anderson chests, and not all of them tribute to some cosmetic surgeon's skill. And we *farangs* have brought about that change, by introducing cheese, pizzas, milk shakes and all sorts of fatty foods into the Thai menu. (Many years ago when Bill Heinecke introduced pizzas into Thailand, everyone said it wouldn't be popular and Bill would go broke. Look at the queues in any Pizza Company store these days and you can see how erroneous that was— on both scores.)

But now let's get back to the traditional Thai food, which I describe as trees and weeds, and the most popular dish of the genre is called *som tam*. Every girl from Northeast Thailand eats this dish. In fact, if they go more than two days without it, they can definitely go loopy! Well my wife does, if nobody else! It is eaten with other vegetables and sticky rice, and the meal is consumed sitting on a mat on the floor. Sitting at a table takes away half the flavour it seems!

If you would like to try this Thai staple, here is a common recipe for this dish. Don't bother trying to count the calories—there aren't any! This is why Northeast girls have to eat every two hours.

Ingredients:

8-12 Thai chillies (bird peppers), each cut into 3-4 segments

8 cloves garlic, peeled and each cut into 2-3 pieces

2 tbsp small dried shrimp

4 cups julienned peeled unripe green papaya, in strips 2-3 inches long and 1/8 inch thick

1 cup cut long beans, 1 1/2-inch-long segments

1 julienned carrot

1/4 cup tamarind juice the thickness of fruit concentrate

Juice of 2-3 limes, to taste

2-3 tbsp fish sauce, to taste

2-3 tbsp palm sugar, melted with 1 tbsp water into a thick syrup—use as needed

2 small tomatoes, cut into bite-size wedges; or 12 cherry tomatoes, halved

1/4 cup chopped unsalted roasted peanuts

Preparation:
Peel the skin off of the papaya, then use a chopper to shred it. The seeds are not used! After you have finished, sprinkle some salt onto the shredded papaya, and let stand for 30 minutes.

Directions:
Now you will need a mortar and pestle. (You can use a regular mixing bowl, but you just don't get the right effect.) Combine all of the ingredients except for the tomato into the mortar bowl and mix thoroughly. Then add the tomato and briefly mix (do not pulverise the tomato into liquid—you want it to be 'bruised' only). Taste check time—if it doesn't burn the roof off your mouth, add more chillies! The effect should be salty, sweet and sour. And hot. And you're welcome to it.

So now you can recognise those girls who eat the traditional Thai food. They're the skinny, two fried egg ones. Trees and weeds will hardly put the weight on. The heavier ones with large bosoms have been hanging around the western culture too long. (Or have a rich boyfriend who bought them a set!)

Fortunately my wife understands that eating *som tam* is an art form that her *farang* husband is unable to master. I will wait until the *som tam* eating mat is folded up and put away for the omelette I have asked for this evening. Fortunately, my wife, who spent a year in five star hotel kitchens, can cook European food. I will never starve.

~

The Dog and the Pickup

THAILAND HAS BECOME THE WORLD'S greatest producer of one-tonne pickups. This is definitely something the country is justifiably proud of, but I have to admit that I have not been pulling my weight here.

I have never actually owned a pickup in my life, but I have owned a cat. These apparently unrelated facts are actually totally dependent upon each other. Read on.

However, before you begin, you must first understand that motor vehicles and I have had a wonderful symbiotic association for many years. We have always needed each other. If my car was indisposed, I became ill with worry. And I am quite sure that when I was too ill to drive, my car would have been agitated too. I have always had faith in my cars. When you race them, you need lots of faith. They can kill you if you don't treat them right!

Now when I use the plural 'cars', I really mean lots of cars. The number of vehicles I have owned (and/

IAIN CORNESS

or raced) exceeds 100, and I gave up counting several years ago. The list includes three Porsche 911s, three Jaguars, two Mazda RX7 rotaries, four Ford Escorts, two Nissan 510s, two Toyota Celicas, 20 MGs, three Chrysler (Dodge) Valiants (one was an ex-ambulance and I believe I was the only doctor in Australia to own his own sick person carrier. Unfortunately, I used mine to tow my race car!) two Ford Customlines, one Mazda MX5, a Dodge Viper, two Ford Falcons, one Holden, seven Isuzu Geminis (six were race cars), two Fiats, one Alfa Romeo GTV 2000—and so the list goes on. I have also owned three Minis, and even one tuk-tuk that I imported from Bangkok into Australia.

As you can see, a very varied list. And you can also see that there's no one-tonne pickups anywhere in that list. Never mind the carrying capacity, there's no pickups at all. Not even in the list of my cars in Thailand. No Isuzus, Chevrolet Colorados, Toyota Vigos, Mazda Fighters, Mitsubishi Stradas, or Ford Rangers. None.

Now there's a good reason for this. For my lifestyle, pickups are totally impractical. Forget about the short cab styles, or even look at extended cabs with tricky concealed suicide doors that carry eight Thai people in comfort, or five foreigners in mild pain. For me, totally impractical.

For starters, how and where do you carry anything? In the tray at the back? Spare me! If it rains, which it often does in this country, anything in the back becomes sodden. No, thank you very much.

But you can always cover the rear section, I can hear you saying from here. My reply is merely this: Why on earth would I do this, when by 1920 we had invented cars with roofs and doors that shut and kept the occupants and contents dry?

Certainly there are times when a roofless one-tonne pickup can be very handy. Transporting predatory giraffes or street elephants that are tired from walking Bangkok's hot and dusty roads immediately spring to mind. However, I must also say that in my past 40 years plus of motoring I have never personally come across the situation described above, though I was witness to the Pattaya Police 'arresting' a baby elephant for soliciting on Beach Road (I think they must have had a complaint from the myriad good-time girls and other creatures that also solicit on Beach Road), and saw them trying to get it on to the tray of a police pickup. Unsuccessfully.

But when I think about it, I also wonder just why we are still making these automotive dinosaurs? After all, the concept is hardly new. In 1917 Ford introduced the Model T One-Tonne truck chassis, its first chassis specifically built for trucks. By 1925 the first factory-assembled Ford pickup made its debut, with a price tag of USD 281. It featured a cargo box, adjustable tailgate, four stake pockets and heavy duty rear springs. Sounds just like the new Ford Ranger, other than the price. They're a little more pricey these days.

But getting back to having a pickup as one's everyday transport. Ignoring the fact that it rains frequently, are you going to leave this vehicle parked outside Kannikar's Karaoke at night, with valuables in the tray? If your cargo is not too hot or too heavy, it will be gone before the engine has cooled down!

Now this is not just a Thailand problem. Pickups, known colloquially as 'utes' (utility trucks), in Australia are also very common. There the farmers have a pickup to transport pigs and cattle fodder (giraffes and elephants are fairly rare Down Under), and although Karaoke bars are thin on the ground in the Northern Territory, cattlemen have been known to pull up outside a pub for an extended session, leaving the ute out the back.

So how do they handle pick-up security in Australia? They've got a dog, that's what! The ubiquitous blue cattle dog that lives in the tray at the back, supercharged nostrils poking forward in the breeze when moving down the highway, stays with the load, and heaven help anyone who puts a hand near it. Bite first, ask questions later, is the blue cattle dog's motto.

So, if they've got everything worked out in Australia, even the rain (there are some parts of Australia that last saw rain before the Queen's coronation in 1952), why did I never own a one-tonne pickup? After all, racing cars need fuel drums, spare wheels and tyres, tools, spare panels and gearboxes and much more lugged to the race circuits, and in Thailand where we are building a house, there's even more to ferry to the building site.

Well, it's simple really. As I mentioned at the beginning, I've always had a cat, and cats and blue cattle dogs have yet to sign a peace pact. You have more chance of the Burmese apologising for knocking down Ayutthya several hundred years ago, than you have of an Aussie blue cattle dog ignoring a cat.

So that, gentle reader, is why my garage does not include a one-tonne pickup!

~

Contracting Rabies

WHILE THAILAND MAY BE THE Land of Smiles, it is also the land of dogs. Millions of them, despite the pooches being given the compulsory 'Home, Rover!' treatment during APEC (Asia-Pacific Economic Cooperation) meetings. If you think I am a victim of self-induced hyperbole, take a quick trip to your local temple. These dogs aren't stupid, they know where they can get a free feed, and their numbers at most times exceed that of worshippers.

Not only are there 10 million dogs in Thailand (the most authoritative figure I could find was given by the Thai Red Cross Society—they arrived at this number by counting the legs and dividing by four) but the incidence of rabid pooches itself is around 30-50 cases a month in Bangkok. The Red Cross estimate of canine numbers in the capital (pre-APEC) was half a million, so with 9.5 million in the provinces, the numbers per month in the country as a whole are much higher.

This is the tale (not 'tail') of what happened to me after being bitten by one of that 9.5 million. This particular animal was unfortunately not a well cared for *canis domesticus*, but one very ill-kempt *soi canis snarlicus aggressivus*.

With the advantage of 20/20 hindsight, I do not totally blame the dog, although I find it difficult in my heart to forgive it. At the time of my meeting with it, it had just been run over by a '*song taew*' and I found later that it had fractured its pelvis and one of its hind legs. It was in no mood for human intervention, no matter how 'well meaning' that intervention might have been.

'Hello puppy dog,' was met with a snarl and a lunge and a sharp toothed grip on my outstretched fingers. My blood and curses were both visible and audible.

Fortunately, my medical training came in handy here, as I immediately instituted the correct first aid for any dog bite. This included washing the wounds with alcohol, and since I was just outside a pub, I found a (possibly better) use for readily available neat Thai whisky. A couple of nips sluiced across the bites was instituted, and to continue the alcohol sterilisation, I applied a liberal quantity to my gastro-intestinal tract, starting at my gullet, administered as immediate first aid. In the meantime, the bowled over Rover was bundled into the back of my vehicle, to be taken to the vet's if it survived the night. It unfortunately did.

The vet was very helpful the next morning, confirming the injuries and adding that he also thought the dog had rabies. Rabies!! Thank you very much, Dr

Vet. This is a lovely disease, which my good book told me is 'invariably fatal once clinical symptoms develop, therefore prevention is of paramount importance.'

Another reference source added the comforting news that the initial symptoms included pain at the site of the bite, (which I had), proceeding to headache (which I could feel coming on), fever, spreading paralysis with episodes of confusion, aggression (I was certainly beginning to feel very aggressive towards Rover), hallucinations and hydrophobia. I already had symptom number one, two and six and I wasn't thirsty. A chill wind blew around me and up my proverbial kilt. In the distance, a rabid dog barked.

That evening I stood there before the mirror, foaming at the mouth while cleaning my teeth, and wondered if I should bite the messenger boy at work as recompense for his terminal laziness. Rabies being invariably fatal! The good book is never wrong.

Of course I had had all my Rabies vaccinations, 'prevention being of paramount importance' (as the good book said again). Had I thump. Like many things that doctors will tell you, sometimes they are a tad too busy to follow the advice themselves. So I was now at risk, and unprotected. The feeling was similar to that of the skydiver who forgot his parachute!

I settled myself and rang the vet again. 'Can you test the dog for Rabies please, and let me know?'

His reply was as cheerful as his initial news. 'Any tests are inconclusive and even examination of the brain post mortem is not 100% certain.'

So much for modern veterinary science, I thought, as I drove to the hospital. You should try sitting in the morning line-up in ER, complete with your medical degrees and listen to the nurses' mutterings as to why I had not been vaccinated before, head hanging in shame and all the rest of it. You want loss of face? This is it!

The post exposure immunisation schedule was necessary of course, and that is a complete course of five injections (after the initial dose, you get more at days 3, 7, 14 and 30).

The injections themselves are not painful, it is the dragging backwards and forwards to the hospital Outpatient clinic that is a pain. That is presuming that you have remembered the appointments. But, being a positive sort of person, you do get to meet some lovely nurses.

I completed the course and so far have suffered no frothing at the mouth, other than at toothbrush time, but the message is there for everyone. Are you protected against *soi canis snarlicus aggressivus* and the Rabies that it might be carrying, that cannot be conclusively diagnosed? The answer is to get yourself vaccinated as a PRE-exposure preventive item. It does make sense. And while you are at it, how is your Tetanus, Polio, Hepatitis A and Hep B? Even if you have had the primary courses for many of these, boosters may also be necessary. See you at the Outpatient's clinic! I'm the chap with the dog hairs.

~

Bins! Bins! Bins!

You can see how long a foreigner has been living in Thailand by the way he says the word 'bills'. If it's 'bins' then he's been here longer than 12 months!

Living here has totally changed my attitude to bills (sorry, bins). In Australia, a country where I spent several decades learning how to speak through my nose, I used to open the mailbox with dread, counting the numbers of bins that I had to pay that month. It was never a fun experience unlocking my Post Office box.

However, in Thailand it is the exact opposite. I sigh with relief when I open the box and get the water bin, telephone bin or any other kind of bin. Why is this? Am I so much more affluent in this country? Quite the contrary. The answer is wrapped up in *Jai yen yen** (calm down) and my attitude to extreme aggravations.

You see, in Australia, there is a completely different mindset towards delinquent bill (sorry bin) payers. The first bin can always be very safely ignored. You'll get another one next month as a reminder. By the third month, the reminder will be in red ink and there will be threats of adding on percentages, but at all times, the owed party will be asking nicely for their money. There will even be a sentence along the bottom saying, 'If you have already paid this amount, please disregard this notice.' Note the 'please' and supplicant attitude.

Even after several months you will only receive a telephone call from a nice lady asking if there is some reason that you haven't paid. Of course there's a reason! You haven't got any money, but neither you, nor they, allude to this. Exhortations to send 'something' are accepted by you and the miserable fraction you send is accepted by them. All very 'matey' as Australia is heavily into mate-ship.

Now let's look at what happens here in Thailand, the Land of Smiles and gentle people who do the *Ramwong* (Thai folk dance) and pour lustral scented water over the hands of their elders (me).

My introduction to the local way of doing things came very early in the piece (when I still used to refer to the accounts as 'bills'). Staggering into the shower one morning, I turned the tap and got nothing. Nada, nix, not a damn drop!

With a towel wrapped around my otherwise naked form, in the interests of public decency, I stumbled out of my front door and asked my neighbour if she had water. Yes, she did, and so did the one on the other side. *Somebody obviously didn't like farangs in the neighbourhood,*

I thought to myself, with typical ex-pat paranoia. *They must have turned my water cock off*, thought I.

I walked outside the gate to turn the handle, and it was gone! So was the entire water meter! My mind was buzzing in disbelief. Who would steal a water meter? It was beyond comprehension.

The answer, as most of the long-stayers will know however, was the Water Department itself! Telephone calls to anyone I knew who could point me in the general direction of why the Water Department wanted their meter back turned up the answer. It seemed that I hadn't paid the bin! Entreaties that I hadn't received a bin for me to pay, fell on deaf ears. My meter was filched, returned to sender, so to speak, and only payment of the outstanding bin, plus a re-connection fee would restore water to my shower hose. And that would be tomorrow! *Jai Yen Yen* lesson number 1.

Being naturally a slow learner with a short attention span and probably incipient Alzheimer's Disease resulted in another bin disaster. I was attempting to ring a business on the Eastern Seaboard to speak with a Mr Wong. Using my mobile, I was eventually answered by a female who asked who I wanted to speak to. I asked for Mr Wong, to be told there was nobody of that name there. I persevered, explaining the Mr Wong I wanted to speak to was from their head office in Taiwan, and I had been assured that he was in their Eastern Seaboard office that morning.

'Who do you think you have rung?' I was then asked. I gave the name of the company (which can remain confidential to protect the guilty), to be told, 'No sir, you are talking to DTAC.'

'Why am I talking to you?' I retorted, wondering why I'd been connected to my mobile phone operator.

'Because you have not paid your telephone bin for two months,' she replied!

Fortunately, by this stage in my life, my Thai wife had taken over supervision of bin paying, and she was able to speak to Ms DTAC and convince her, Thai to Thai, that we had not received any bins, but we would pay immediately. Mind you, it turned out that only one month's bin had not been received or paid, because as the time comes up towards sending off the next bin, they just divert your outgoing calls to themselves. Pay in time or be damned forever to ringing DTAC for fun and pleasure, and forget Mr Wong (remembering always that two Wongs do not make a White).

I am getting smarter in my dotage, now getting the bank to make sure the Water Department doesn't abscond with their meter, and my wife has the calendar ringed on the dates we should get the phone bins. But it is always a relief to see that box, stuffed with bins, since I have failed *Jai Yen Yen* yet again!

Which reminds me, I don't remember seeing the electric bin this month! Been nice chatting with you, but I really should go now and search the PO box. 'Check bin!' Thank you.

~

*Publisher's note: '*Jai yen yen*' literally means 'cool your heart'. If a Thai sees a friend becoming angry and emotional, he/she will urge them to '*jai yen yen*' because it is not Thai-ish to lose your temper.

~

Birth Certificates

As EX-PATS WE OFTEN FEEL that we are burdened with an enormous amount of paperwork, any time we have to do something involving any Thai government department. Those who doubt this should try marrying a Thai or even just getting a Thai driving license.

However, it would be wrong to think that this is a situation peculiar to Thailand. Government red tape is particularly strong, no matter which country it is made in. For example, after living in Australia for 40 years, much pressure was being put upon me to take out Australian citizenship. After two separate attempts at filling out the forms, I gave up. I only have three tertiary degrees and it was beyond me. Perhaps the Vietnamese boat people get given a 'master sheet' and they all crib off that?

But I digress. My baby daughter is eligible for UK citizenship, since I was born in the UK. I made the trip to Bangkok to visit the UK folks to inquire as to what I would need to do this. The young lady was very helpful and I was furnished with the Registration of Birth Application Forms. The second page even showed the required documents that would need to be seen. This was looking too simple. This was later shown to be a pipe dream.

In essence I needed to bring along baby Marisa's local birth certificate and translation thereof. I also needed my passport, birth certificate and divorce certificate and a translation if needed, plus my wife's passport and birth certificate and finally our marriage certificate and its translation.

After several days, I managed to find most of the required documentation, other than my original birth certificate, but I did have a photocopy.

Once more I set off for Bangkok and proudly advanced to the window and presented everything to the very pleasant young lady. She ticked everything off, until we came to my birth certificate. Did I not have it? No, I explained that there was a photocopy, and the details in my passport verified my place of birth and the date.

She scurried away to ask for advice. Back she came to say that the photocopy was not good enough (despite the passport) and I would have to get an original. She smiled sweetly and gave me an advice form, and said that I could do it over the phone and even use credit/debit cards to pay for it. With a sigh of resignation, I left.

I rang the UK number, to be told by the disembodied voice that I was placed in a queue and I was number 19. For the next few days, I tried again, and gave up again when informed of the queue. I then got smarter and worked out when the office would open in the UK and rang one minute later. Success!

A government official asked me for my name and where I was born. 'Lisburn,' said I. 'Lisbon?' said Mr UK government official. 'That's in Portugal.'

I assured him that I was aware of that fact, but I was born in Lisburn, in Northern Ireland.

'Oh, you have to ring the office in Northern Ireland,' said he, but did at least furnish me with their telephone number.

Once again it was ring and queue, ring and queue, until I eventually I spoke with an Irish lady, whose accent was particularly broad, indicating she was indeed the genuine article. Once again we went through the routine:

'Do you know your full name?' I was asked.

Yes I did, and I also knew the date of my birth.

'Do you know who your father was?'

Again I did. And I knew I was born in the Lisburn hospital.

'Do you know who your mother was?'

I smiled. Yes I did, and her maiden name. The next question almost floored me.

'Do you know where your mother was when you were born?'

Yes, she was lying right there with me in the hospital bed in Lisburn! The next question beat it hollow.

'Are you sure you weren't adopted?'

By now I was starting to get a little testy, but it seemed I had convinced her that I was really a Lisburn lad (even though I sounded like an Aussie). Then came payment.

'I will use a debit card,' I said.

'I'm sorry, but we don't accept debit cards.'

'But it says here on my bit of paper from your embassy that you do!'

'I'm sorry, we don't, but we'll take a credit card.'

Not having a credit card (by choice, I might add) I told her to hang on, while I got a friend's American Express Gold card.

'I'm sorry, but we don't accept American Express,' said the Irish brogue. I would have to ring back.

It was back to the ring and queue for a couple of days, but eventually I did manage it. This time, with a mate's Mastercard. Painstakingly she took down the numbers, then said, 'I'm sorry but the numbers are wrong.'

'Madam, I have the card in my hand and the numbers are correct.'

It was to no avail.

On the following day I rang again, with yet another credit card. This time the numbers were right, but she needed to speak to the holder, in this case my Thai secretary. I passed the phone over. She passed it back after a minute's blankness.

'I can't understand what she's saying,' said the secretary. Since I was having trouble understanding the Irish brogue, I could appreciate the Thai girl's dilemma. I became interpreter for both, and finally the transaction was completed.

So yes, I do now possess a Certified Copy of an Entry of Birth relating to myself, and one day, when I am feeling strong enough, I must go up to Bangkok and register my baby daughter's birth. Hopefully that will be before she finishes university!

~

To Market, To Market, to Buy a Fat Pig

THERE WAS A NURSERY RHYME we used to sing that went:
'To market, to market, to buy a fat pig,
Home again, home again, jiggety jig.'

Remember it? I am sure you do. However, in the ever more sophisticated Western world, you will be hard pressed these days to find a market where you can buy the aforementioned porker, unless you have a livestock license (should that be a deadstock license I wonder?) and a letter of authority from the National Ministry of Pigs.

Markets in Thailand, however, are a totally different style of porcine commerce. I refer specifically to the local market, called the '*talad sod*', the local 'fresh' market.

Now, if you do not know where your local *talad sod* is located, then shame on you! You are missing out on one of the genuine Thai institutions, but one where you (and me), as foreigners, can go and indulge and enjoy some local customs, without being ripped off and without double-pricing to get into. No double pricing! Please don't tell the Interior Ministry of Selective Prices, or it will all be changed next week!

I was introduced to 'our' *talad sod* by my wife, who decried my shopping habits as soon as she read the supermarket labels on the polystyrene-trayed and plastic-wrapped meats I kept in the refrigerator, during our courting days.

'You pay too mut,' was just one of her remarks after looking at the contents of my fridge, and the expiry dates which were closer to a historical record of leaving the abattoir, than a suggestion of 'use by'.

And so, for those of you who have not had the luck to go to a local market, I present the Soi Watboonkanjana Talad Sod. This market is probably reasonably upmarket compared to those in the villages, in that it is fully covered above and fully concreted below, but the concept is identical. Sellers rent table space and buyers flock in for all their domestic needs.

There appears to be a loose categorisation of the sections, with most (but not all) of the seafood in one area. Ditto the meats, vegetables, cooked items, fruit, appliances, videos, CDs, clothing and toys. Of course, not forgetting the newspapers and periodicals, though I admit I am yet to find an English language publication on the shelves at Soi Watboonkanjana!

However, the immediate impression to the untrained eye, is that there is order (somehow) in the chaos. My wife seems to know it, as she plunges confidently into the seething mass of buyers and sellers, to disappear from view very quickly. From my elevated Western eye view, it is very difficult to spot 'my' short lady with black hair, from all the other short ladies with black hair. However, 6-foot-tall *farang*s with white hair and big noses are easy to find.

I have to say that I do enjoy going to our market, just looking and wondering at what I will find next. The range of goods available beats Tesco-Lotus and Carrefour hollow. (Perhaps they should send their highly paid marketing people to Soi Watboonkanjana for an object lesson in purchaser's preferences?)

For example, live eels seem to be in short supply in the international supermarket chains, or perhaps they are always sold out before I get there. Fried tasty insect nibbles are also not offered from the supermarket shelves of the multinationals, but the local market can supply these snacks with drinks. There are also bottles of alcoholic drinks that appear to have no labels, but obviously the local residents know what they are. I should, in the defence of the multinationals, say that I am happier with a bottle of Veuve Clicquot (even non-vintage) from Carrefour, than a bottle of strange brown alcoholic liquid from Soi Watboonkanjana! But then, much of that may come from my upbringing, which was not champagne satiated, but at least champagne stimulated!

Far from being filthy and flea infested, as many *farang*s would imagine, our local market is (comparatively) very clean. The vendors wave their sticks with plastic bags tied to the end to scare away the flies, while the fresh fish are kept on and under ice. Even the meat is kept cool and the 'butcher' wears a plastic glove. The fishmonger even wraps our selection in paper lined with plastic. Undoubtedly the international health and hygiene inspectorate might have a field day, but I have to say that our market does try hard, and I have only once suffered from a dose of Montezuma's Revenge, or Bangkok Belly as we call it here, where I could lay the blame fairly at the feet of the local market, after eating some oysters.

No discourse on local markets is complete without some mention of price. These are plainly displayed, and often there are trays with three or six items together, and you choose the tray you want. All very above board, and self selected. Trips to the supermarket for vegetables, fish, prawns, and meat for the day usually means a withdrawal of 500 baht from my long-suffering wallet to feed my enlarging family. A trip to the local market to pick up the same items, seems to result in change being returned from 200 baht. I can feel my Scottish forebears nodding in approval!

Oh yes, I did mention the fat pig, didn't I? You can certainly purchase a fat porker here. Neatly dissected and bisected, with the heads and tails together on one table, and other cuts on another. For the really professional pig fanciers, there is yet another table with all sorts of internal bits that no self-respecting pig would ever have wanted to have on display, and I certainly wouldn't want displayed on my dining table either.

But somebody must buy all these livers and lungs, or else the seller would not be there. Local markets work completely on the principle of supply and demand, though that really should be 'demand and supply' to be more appropriate.

Now, has anybody seen my wife? She's about 5 foot 2 inches tall, with long black hair, last seen at the coconut stall ...

~

The *talad sod*, the local fresh market, is a genuine Thai institution. No double-pricing for *farangs* means you can buy delicious, fresh food at local prices.

Mongolian Blue Spot

Let me present you with a medical mystery. One that has been discussed for over 1,000 years, and one that you too can become involved in. Or you may even be one of the 'sufferers' yourself. And doing the detective work in Thailand could even be fun.

So to the facts. Bruises on a child's body are often considered proof that a baby has been battered. An apparent bruise on the buttocks, the shape of a hand and five fingers seems like 'undeniable' proof. In fact, there was a very celebrated instance of a GP in the UK having discovered that so many of the Asian babies in his practice were showing signs of being 'battered' that the children's welfare people were called in and an enormous number of children taken away. However, the highly observant GP was wrong!

In Thailand, and the rest of Asia, a newborn baby with the 'handprint' bruise is very common, while child abuse is not common at all. The problem, or rather the condition, relates back to Genghis Khan and the Mongol hordes. It is a wonderful piece of folklore and also a fine example of applied genetics.

Let's look at the folklore first—and you are going to have to dig very deep to get this tale anywhere else! A Mongolian baby, called Tanujin, was born just over 1,000 years ago, but did not breathe. His father, in desperation, held his newborn son upside down and smacked him severely over the bottom, so much so that the baby drew breath and lived, but carried the life-giving bruise for the rest of his days. That baby later became Genghis Khan, (which means King of the Earth), and by the time he died in 1227 he was the ruler of a large chunk of it, including the area which later became known as Thailand. And in case you think that is mainly an exaggeration, Alexander the Great was considered to be the greatest ruler of all time, but in terms of amount of land conquered he possessed one quarter of the area that Genghis Khan ruled over.

History has chronicled that Khan's Mongol hordes raped, pillaged and annexed countries from China to Persia. His highly mobile troops travelled the difficult terrain of Siberia. Famous cities were captured and looted, such as Tashkent, Baghdad (still a good place to stay away from, thanks George) and Bokhara. Cities that surrendered were spared but those that resisted were razed and the people slaughtered. The Mongols conquered northern India and Afghanistan. In 1222, they defeated the Russian and Bulgarian armies. At the time of Genghis Khan's death, his empire stretched from China's Yellow River to the Dnieper, in Russia.

And now back to some interesting folklore. The descendants of Genghis Khan also showed the hand-shaped bruise on the buttocks, beginning with his four sons Ogdai, Jagatai, Juji and Tule, who were given one quarter of the empire each after their father died. They in turn passed on this 'trademark' and so this continues till today. If your Eurasian children have the sign of Genghis Khan, call it Mongolian Blue Spot, and you can claim descent from the warrior king. However, there is quite a number of you, so I think there won't be much left in Genghis' estate by today.

Now, Mongolian Blue Spot, as a clinical condition, is well documented, and I came across figures suggesting that at least one Mongolian spot is present on over 90% of Native Americans and people of African descent, over 80% of Asians, over 70% of Hispanics, and just under 10% of fair-skinned infants (Clinical Paediatric Dermatology, 1993).

Medically we describe Mongolian Blue Spot as flat bluish to bluish grey skin markings that commonly appear at birth (or shortly thereafter) and scientifically they are called Congenital Dermal Melanocytosis, or just Dermal Melanocytosis. They are flat, pigmented lesions with nebulous borders and irregular shape. They appear commonly at the base of the spine, on the buttocks and back, but can also appear as high as the shoulders and elsewhere.

The medical textbooks also warn that occasionally, Mongolian Blue Spots are mistaken for bruises and questions about child abuse arise. Obviously a textbook that the UK GP did not read! Mongolian Blue Spots are birthmarks, not bruises.

Now, do not forget that this condition is alternatively known as Congenital Dermal Melanocytosis. When you remember that Genghis and the rape and pillage lads went through Russia (and the Mongol peoples there went through to North America), and a fair bit of seed would have been spilled in France, Germany and Spain on the way there, it looks as if there really could be a Mongol-influenced gene pool in which the Europeans could pick up some genetic inheritance. In fact, there is one area in France where almost every child has Mongolian Blue Spot. (So much for ethnic purity!)

Now I have an (unverified) quote from *American Journal of Human Genetics* (2003): 'We have identified a Y-chromosomal lineage with several unusual features. It was found in 16 populations throughout a large region of Asia, stretching from the Pacific to the Caspian Sea, and was present at high frequency. The pattern of variation within the lineage suggested that it originated in Mongolia around 1,000 years ago. Such a rapid spread cannot have occurred by chance; it must have been a result of selection. The lineage is carried by likely male-line descendants of Genghis Khan, and we therefore propose that it has spread by a novel form of social selection resulting from their behaviour.'

(One has to smile at the geneticist's use of 'a novel form of social selection resulting from their behaviour,' a wonderful English euphemism for the rape and pillage scene!)

So, for all of you with children with a peculiar blue birthmark on their bottoms, or for those interested in checking friends and neighbours (or the young ladies dancing in the chrome pole palaces), it seems as though the lineage can be verified. You really have found descendants of the man who conquered more of the world than Alexander the Great.

However, all of us have to die one day, and possession of the Mongolian Blue Spot does not imply immortality. Genghis Khan, it is said, fell off his horse and was killed, but he was 65 years old at the time of his demise. In those days, that was a very long life. At his funeral, 40 maidens were burned to death as an offering to his spirit and as a celebration of his life.

Some of these poor women may have thought they had survived the worst of it once they found out Genghis was dead, only to find out that he had a plan for them after he had fallen. It was tough being a maiden in those days!

~

Driving Test

THAILAND'S ECONOMY IS MAINLY PROPPED up by different sections of the Thai industry, depending upon which paper you read or which politician you listened to this week.

There are those who say Thailand is still 60% an agri-economy, whereas our ex-PM would rather have us thinking smarter and being the IT hub of Asia, the world and following that, the universe.

However, after spending one day at the local driver's licensing authority, and then harking back to 'minor' details such as those involved with work permits and visas, I can assure you that Thailand's economy is propped up by the photocopy industry.

This earth-shattering concept was really brought home when my good lady, the lovely Som, decided she wanted to sit her driving test. Personally being someone who considers that driving is an 'art form' I had visions of Learner Permits and many afternoons with L plates affixed to the family vehicle while I grunted and gears were graunched. Silly me! This is Thailand!

It appears that the concept of a Learner's Permit has not yet reached these shores. In Thailand you learn to drive anonymously and then sit your test. There are those churlish enough to say you buy your license first and learn to drive later, but I am sure that in this, the newly rehabilitated Thailand, such nefarious practices could not possibly exist!

However, I decided I should approach my friendly insurer to get cover for the young lady while learning. Ah, shock number two. If the driver of the car does not hold a license, then all insurance is null and void! I explained the situation—I would be in the passenger's seat at all times while the learner was under instruction, so surely the cover would be there?

'No, I'm sorry,' was the response.

'So what happens in the case of an accident?' I asked.

'Swap seats,' was the helpful reply!

In the face of this Thai conundrum, which I obviously was not going to solve, I turned the tuition over to a Thai driving school. How they cope with the insurance problem is beyond me—but it was their problem—not mine! Mine was to come later.

After 26 hours of instruction behind the wheel of a venerable Toyota Corolla, the instructor said that Som was ready to sit the driving test. However, she had to supply her own vehicle.

The BIG DAY was a Tuesday, so I let the office know I would be in a little later, and I drove to the testing centre, with the aspiring new driver in the passenger seat. Som had decided she wanted to get a motorcycle license at the same time, which seemed a reasonable request. Both theory tests were done by the same officer and the test drive track was the same for both two and four wheels. Being Thai, Som needed a copy of her House Registration papers, a copy of her ID card and we threw in a copy of her passport for good measure, to go along with the required size photograph. We had everything.

It was necessary for us to get there at 9am for the 10am start, as we had been advised there were some forms to be filled in. We presented ourselves at the window and were given two copies of the application forms. One for car. One for bike. They were the same forms! However, there was no 'tick the boxes for license requested'. Both forms had to be filled out.

The duly filled forms were presented at the window, for us to be told the House Registration papers and ID card copies had to be duplicated again for each application.

'Amazingly' just outside the compound was a row of shops, all bristling with state of the art photocopiers. I ran over, as time was getting short, and it was worse than Patpong Road, with women all trying to drag me into their shop for the necessary photocopying. I chose one, had the documents photocopied again and rushed back, just in time for Som to hand in the two completed, and getting thicker, bundles.

Ah, not so fast! Each photocopy had to be signed, and Thai signatures take a little while, with the names being as long as they are. By the time that was accomplished, Som was a tad late, but she was allowed into the examination room to sit the written multiple-choice test, after the video on rules and regulations.

However, since she wanted two licenses, she had to sit the written test twice! In the meantime, I sat outside trying to read the Thai script above the windows, while watching the steady stream of applicants leaving the exam room. They all finished before lunchtime, as they were only sitting for one license! The testing lady took pity on Som and allowed her to sit in the office filling out test number 2 while the staff all went to lunch. By now I had been sitting on my bench so long I was about to ask if I had any letters when the postman came through.

Having finished, Som was allowed out when the staff returned and we raced over the road to find something to eat at the local photocopy shop, which did food as well as photocopies. It was by now after 2pm.

We returned to the testing centre where the officer was wading through the multiple photocopied forms. We waited. We waited. We waited, while I practised *jai yen yen* and Som got frustrated at the delays. By this stage I was in a state of semi-hibernation, so it didn't matter anymore.

By 3pm and six hours on the bench for me, Som was eventually told she could have the practical test, and bring her car round to the start of the test route at the rear of the building. Eventually she was tested and passed, but there was not enough time for the motorcycle test, because the centre was closing!

'Please come back another day, and bring all your photocopied documents.'

Now I know where the logs go from the illegal logging in the Salween Dam area. They are used to feed photocopiers!

~

On Being a Squid

HAVE YOU EVER THOUGHT THAT you might once have been a squid?

In this country, where reincarnation is considered normal, it is not beyond the bounds of credibility. With my kind of past life, I think I'd probably be lucky to even get that far up the food chain!

This was not morbid esoteric mental net-casting that got me to this reflection on the humble squid, but more a reflection on life from the safety of my local roadside eatery.

This conundrum all stems from my in-built belief in routines. Especially in the mornings.

Being a night person, mornings are not greeted with pleasure or alacrity, but can be muddled through by applying the age-old principle of rote. Leaving one's clothes in the same place for the morning dressing means that one can actually greet the new day wearing a semblance of correct clothing, but misplaced keys from the night before verges on a national disaster.

After the clothes dressing routine, the next hurdle to be tripped over is breakfast. In my past life (in Australia and post-squid) I used to point the car in the direction of the closest fast-food outlet that served breakfast. It was unimportant what the offering called 'breakfast' really consisted of. The important feature was that they served you something in a ready-to-eat form.

I did not have to add hot water, whisk anything, find the plates, the milk or even the fridge. They did it all for me. 'Here is your nosebag full of food. Put it on and have a happy breakfast!'

After coming to Thailand to live, there was an immediate problem. There was no fast-food outlet on the way to the office! However, there was the local noodle lady, and it became obvious that I would have to train her in the gentle art of breakfast making. After a week of asking for *'guaytiew naam moo Daeng,'* my preferred start-of-day snack of noodle soup and red pork, she began to understand that the morning routine had become set in stone. No longer was it necessary to vocalise the request.

After I sat down, a steaming bowl of my daily order, and a bottle of soda water with a straw, were placed before me. 'Here is your nosebag full of food. Put it on and have a happy (Thai) breakfast!' Noodle shop ladies are truly special people.

One morning, while staring out over the rim of my noodle soup and trying out the focus capabilities of my eyes, I came across another routine. Pulling up outside the noodle shop was the local fishmonger on wheels. This came as a battered, decrepit motorcycle complete with sidecar and a rider of the same description. But what was even more interesting was the 'catch of the day'. In a large black plastic bucket were squid. Shoals of them.

Several noodle shop ladies descended upon the squid saleslady. Squid were selected carefully after much detailed examination that included lifting them up, poking them and whatever other tests one does on squid destined for the soup pot.

Now, for me, I have to admit that all squid look the same (though they might say the same about us) and I am sure that Mother Squid cannot pick out her own squidlets in the shoals, but these squid were examined minutely.

Considering that each one would end up chopped up into little coiled rubbery bits that live in the bottom of a bowl of *tom yum talay*, this appeared to me to be somewhat of an overkill situation. But then, I have never been a noodle lady.

But this morning ritual was not yet over. Much bartering and haggling ensued until an amicable agreement had been reached and money changed hands to the accompaniment of much laughing. My noodle lady returned smiling. The bargain must have gone her way. The squid ritual was complete.

My breakfast nosebag being empty at this stage, I was more able to indulge in cognitive thought, and I began to think more about the morning squid routine.

This was obviously not a one-off situation, but one where I was witnessing a time-honoured interplay. The squid lady and the noodle shop cooks were all playing a part that probably went back several thousands of squid generations, depending upon what is the average reproductive age of your average squid.

This was not discussed at Zoology 1, so I have to profess ignorance. Even Google didn't seem to have this stored away for electronic retrieval, other than on the one hit which ended up (maddeningly) as 'The page you have requested has expired'—a message you will all be too familiar with I am sure.

My mind began to drift again and I could see the primeval squid seller trudging up from the boat on the beach, to sell her squid to the awaiting housewives and noodle ladies. I could see a lifestyle where the most stressful part of the day was selecting the best squid.

We should not forget this with our ceaseless quest for sophistication. Several generations of squid sellers cannot be wrong! I began to see it all so clearly that I could understand that even being a 'faceless' squid could have an impact on the society of yesteryear, and still to that of today—and also tomorrow.

So as you drive past the noodle lady on the corner of your street, think about the little rubbery bits in the bottom of the bowl. They have had their own part to play in the overall scheme of our society, and despite looking a lot like their brother and sister squids, that might have been me and you in a previous incarnation!

~

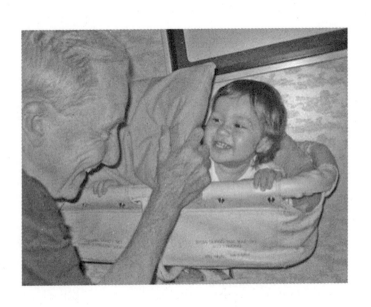

Second Time Dads

I WAS AWOKEN LAST SUNDAY morning by my three-year-old daughter climbing all over me, shouting, 'Brekfuss, brekfuss!' in my ear. This reminded me of just how lucky I am to be a Second Time Dad.

In Thailand, there are many Second Time Dads, and a much higher percentage than there is in the West. There are many reasons for this, but principally it boils down to cultural differences. The West has espoused a 'youth' culture, whilst in the East there is still respect for the elders. The end result is that in the West, by the time you reach 40 you have had it, mate. Your marriage has long since fallen apart. The courts gave her the kids, but you get the bills. Lucky you!

What you have to live with is the fact that you're over the hill. Nobody wants you. The job market doesn't want your years of experience, and as for Western women? They won't give you a second glance, let alone a second chance. Celebrate your 41st birthday at home by yourself, with your pipe and slippers. And the dog. If the dog still likes you. And don't wait for a birthday card from your children. It won't come.

Now, in Thailand, the ex-pat *farang*s do tend to be an older group. In fact many are pensioners from the UK, Australia, the US and other far points west. With their pensions they can eke out their life back home feeding shillings into the gas meter, with the high point of existence being a beer in the local pub with similarly afflicted old codgers every Friday night. Since I have never been in that group, I have no idea what they discuss, but euthanasia wouldn't be a bad start.

However, some of them find their way to Thailand. They find that their pension is enough for them to live on quite comfortably. And it is warm enough that you don't need shillings for the gas meter!

They also find that there are many young ladies here in Thailand who do not scorn them because they are old, but are quite happy to spend time with them (and help them spend their pension allowance as well, it should be pointed out)!

Now setting up house with one of the obliging ladies from the beer bar will certainly give them company. But it is often a case of 'buy one, get two free' as most of the bar ladies have at least one, and generally two children being cared for by Mamma in the village. Again there are many societal reasons for this, but the Thai men from the village, who got them pregnant in the first place, are not known for fidelity.

So our pensioners become surrogate Second Time Dads, and many of them do a sterling job, educating their stepchildren and giving them an otherwise undreamed of chance for the future.

There are also the other *farangs* who have come here to live and work. Like most males, they yearn for female company, but many shy away from beer bar liaisons, and prefer to meet interesting women from their workplace or similar meeting grounds. There can be quite an age disparity here too, and it is to this group of Second Time Dads that I belong.

Before my wife and I got married, we discussed everything from koalas to contraception. With 30+ years between us, there was much that worried me. Not being able to offer her even a vague possibility of 50 years of marriage was just one. However, with true Thai practicality she said, 'Why are you worrying about being older than me? I am the one who will get left, not you, and I am willing to accept it.'

Then came the subject of children. My eldest son, Dr Jonathan Corness, of whom I am inordinately (and unjustly) proud, is now in his 30s. His mother has to take all the credit for raising him; I just supplied the gene pool for him to splash around in. But did I want any more children?

On the other hand, my prospective Thai bride had had no children. Was I justified in saying, just because I had had children, that she should be denied? The answer was obviously no. So it was left that if children came (and if I was still firing bullets and not just blanks) that was fine. But if no children were to result from our union, then that would also be fine.

It was the first fine. Now we have two children, and that is enough, thank you, as I have to plan for many coming years of expensive schooling, but being a Second Time Dad is honestly really wonderful. You are no longer working incredibly long hours, struggling to build businesses, houses and deal with overdrafts. You can come home at reasonable hours. You are also far more flexible in your attitudes. A certain maturity comes out of aging. A maturity that helps you deal with young people growing up.

And all that gets me back to 'brekfuss'. Every Sunday morning I reserve for my daughter Marisa and myself. We sort out the clothes for the laundry and then set off to have breakfast together somewhere, where she sits proudly next to her Dad and tries different *farang* foods from my plate. Then we exchange the dirty laundry for the freshly washed and ironed clothes and come home and together we hang the items in the wardrobe.

It is perhaps terribly mundane, but actually wonderfully heart-warming and bonding. I have been given a second chance at helping a little person become an adult in a loving family.

Of course, as soon as her baby brother Evan is old enough, I will have to put a special time aside for him too. Sunday lunch sounds good at this stage.

~

Appried Ringuistics

I HAVE ALWAYS BEEN A fan of linguistics. For those who study ancient languages, they can, like an unfolding detective novel, see the migration and integration of peoples throughout the ages, and the Thai language is just one of these.

We are categorised as one of the Tai speaking nations. It is this study that explains just why Yunnan folk in China speak a type of what I shall loosely call 'Thai' and there are many people in Thailand who have descended from the 'Tais'.

Transliteration from the national language into English in this country is also difficult. I shall on purpose ignore the large Laos speaking contingent from Isan, whose dulcet tones can be heard shrieking from any beer bar in Pattaya, after a customer has turned down their never-to-be-repeated offers. And '*Sawatdi Baw*' to all you young ladies!

Transliteration here, can only be a well-educated guess at best, with a 44 consonant alphabet on one side and a 26 character English alphabet on the other. This goes a long way towards explaining why you will see many English spellings of Thai place names. None of them are incorrect! Or put another way, Chomthian, Jomtien and Chomtien all refer to the next beach after Pattaya. Take any bus to one of those three destinations and you will end up 50 metres from my house. Guaranteed!

However, although I don't really give a tinker's curse about how Jomtien is spelled (or spelt, if you come from the US of A) or transliterated, I do take a more than passing interest in how my daughter's name is written down! And this really is a tale of the Real Thailand!

When she was born, it was supposed to happen on a Wednesday, and my wife, being a good and traditional Thai lady had the book that gave suitable names that corresponded to days of the week.

Following the Caesarean operation, baby Corness, who was now renamed Arisa to be a Tuesday girl, was brought into the world that one day early. However, it became fairly evident, very early in the piece, that native Thai speakers were having a problem saying 'Arisa', and 'Alisa' would be heard at least 50% of the time.

This was not a problem, said my wife, as everyone gets a nickname in Thailand. Perhaps this might be so, but I vetoed every nickname that was put forward by my Thai in-laws. So at six months of age, baby Arisa, remained Ar(l)isa, until a party held at my mad mate

Peewee's house. (Peewee I am keeping as a subject for another book.)

Another guest was a fortune teller, and since my wife is still a traditional Thai lady, words that come from fortune tellers are veritable pearls of wisdom, cast before the swine. Fortune teller said there were not enough letters in the name Arisa Corness—we needed one more, so an M was placed in front to make Marisa Corness. Problem solved. Err, not quite.

You see, the name Arisa had already been registered on her birth certificate, so we needed to 'officially' change her name. 'Easy,' said my wife again. But as any person who has lived in Thailand for more than three minutes knows, there is nothing here that is quite that 'easy'.

Away we trotted and explained to the person behind the desk at the City Hall that this little baby was now to be called 'Marisa'.

'No problems,' said the name-change department chief. 'What name again?'

'Marisa,' we repeated. So away went the lady with the paperwork and we returned the following day to pick it all up, and the English translation that was included. There we were presented with the certificate containing the new name for my daughter. Now officially in all records as 'Malisa Corness'!

When I pointed this out to my wife, I was again told 'No problem. Thai people will say it as Marisa, anyway.'

So if one day in the future Marisa wonders why her name is actually Malisa, I will refer her to a book on linguistics. Hopefully she will forgive us.

However, one of the more interesting linguistic frauds has been dropped on the unsuspecting world by the Russians. Yes, that strange language, laced with strange characters so that Anglo-Saxons have no chance of being able to read, or fathom, what the Russians are doing. Gentle readers, the Russian language is a sham!

Let me explain. Do you remember, as a child, making up codes? The simplest was just to give each letter of the alphabet a number, so that A was 1 and B was 2 and so forth. So 'BAD' was written '214' and we could communicate with our friends in secret, and our parents would not know. Well that was the concept anyway.

Those codes still exist today, and Russian is actually only English, but written in code! Far fetched? Not at all. Walk down any street in Thailand that has a Russian restaurant, and you will see a sign saying 'PECTOPAH'. Fiendish Russians!

Now here is the code: all P's are R's, all C's are S and all H's are N's. So PECTOPAH becomes P(R)EC(S)TORAH(N). PECTOPAH then reads as RESTORAN in Russian, and RESTORAN is really close enough to RESTAURANT for me!

Need more proof? Remember the days of the great Russian Olympic lady shot-putters? The 'ladies' who didn't sit down to pee, it is rumoured. What was emblazoned on the back of their tracksuits? It was

CCCP, which did not make any sense as an acronym, until you apply the code and you get SSSR, which stood for the Soviet Socialist States of Russia (or something similar). Russian is a straight-out con! Don't be fooled in future, appry ringuistics (sorry, apply linguistics) and the Kremlin is yours! (You can have it. I don't want it!)

~

Cancer in the Tropics

CANCER IS THE ONE MEDICAL condition that the expat fears most. Coming to terms with cancer, whilst being an alien in a foreign land, can be difficult. It is a time when you need family and old friends, but unfortunately, they are 'over there' and you are 'over here'. And for things medical, you don't have the local GP (general practitioner) who speaks your language. It is easy to feel alone.

This week, three of my friends contacted me to say they had just been diagnosed as having prostate cancer. They range in age between 50 and 70. One has already had the operation to remove the prostate gland completely, the second is waiting till November to have his prostate removed, while the third has gone to Europe, hoping for a magical cure. Unfortunately, he will find there isn't one.

Prostate cancer is also extremely common; something that we men have to live with. After all, our women are always telling us how lucky we are to be men and not to have to go through childbirth, for example, so it's probably only right and equitable that there is a male downside. In fact this year in the United States, almost 180,000 men will be told that they have prostate cancer. That's 180,000 downsides.

With all our older friends getting prostate problems, does this mean there is a rise in the incidence? Has the urbanised world or greenhouse gasses struck us all a death blow? Or is it just underpants that are too tight? Simple answer—No! One reason for the 'apparent' increase in prostate cancer is the fact that prostate cancer is a disease of aging, and thankfully, we are all living longer. The statistics would show that by age 50, almost 50% of American men will have microscopic signs of prostate cancer. By age 75, almost 75% of men will have some cancerous changes in their prostate glands. Do the maths. By 100, we've all got it!

So does this mean that life really ends at around 76? Fortunately, no. Most of these cancers stay within the prostate, producing no signs or symptoms, or are so slow-growing that they never become a serious threat to health.

The good news is that in other words, you die of something else before the prostate gets you! You die with it, rather than from it. It may be a sobering thought to all you sprightly chaps who are still 10 foot tall and bullet-proof that despite all medical research and advances, the death rate will always be the same— one per person. We all have to die of something—even me—and I just hope it isn't from boredom! That would be a real killer.

While the numbers quoted above look fearsome, the real situation is not quite so bad. A much smaller number of men will actually be treated for prostate cancer. About 16% of American men will be diagnosed with prostate cancer during their lives; 8% will develop significant symptoms; but only 3% will die of the disease. Put another much more positive way, 97% won't die from prostate cancer. This means I must be OK, as my three friends hopefully make up the 3% of my acquaintances.

While prostate cancer can be 'aggressive', breaking out from the prostate gland itself and attacking other tissues, including brain and bone, fortunately this is the minority scenario. The great majority of prostate cancers are slow growing, and it can be decades between the early diagnosis and the cancer growing large enough to produce symptoms.

So let's look at diagnosis and get the 'blood test' out of the way first. The blood test is called Prostate Specific Antigen, or PSA for short (we medicos love acronyms). Up until then we had another acronymical test called DRE (digital rectal examination), which, quite frankly, was not all that popular.

As medical students, we were taught: 'If you don't put your finger in it, you'll put your foot in it!' Despite this, 'buyer resistance' was high, so when news came through about a 'blood test', millions of men began rejoicing and the sale of rubber gloves plummeted.

Unfortunately, PSA is not a go / no go test. A normal range test doesn't guarantee you haven't got it, and an elevated result doesn't automatically mean that you are about to claim early on your life insurance (or your dependants, anyway).

However, there is good news. We are becoming smarter with the PSA test. Elevated PSA levels in the blood correlate roughly with the volume of cancer in the prostate, with the stage and grade of the tumour, and with the presence or absence of cancer metastases or growths in other tissues. Serial PSA examinations can also show the rate of this growth; another good reason for regular check-ups.

Like many other cancers, prostate cancer can only be fully diagnosed by examining prostate tissue samples under the microscope. When your doctor suspects prostate cancer on the basis of your symptoms, or the results of a clever finger rectal examination (DRE), and / or a PSA test, the definitive diagnosis will need a biopsy.

So let's imagine that now you have had a positive biopsy. You've got it! What are the real options? Actually very many, and they depend mainly upon the 'stage' of the cancer and your age at the time of diagnosis.

'Staging' has four main grades. Stage 1 cannot be felt and is diagnosed through pathological testing. Stage II can be felt, but it is confined to the prostate. Stage III is coming out of the gland and Stage IV has grown into nearby tissues.

Treatment can be 'watch and wait', surgery, radiation, hormone therapy, eating herbs or muttering mantras. Often it will be a combination of some of the above (but I'd forget the mantras, if I were you). Cancer can't hear.

This is where you need to discuss your options with your doctor. If you are a young man with stage IV, then you have to make up your mind quickly. But if you are 75 with stage I or II, then you have more time, as you will most likely die of other causes before the prostate cancer gets you.

'Watch and wait' has much going for it, but you must be prepared to get to know your urologist on first name terms. You will be seeing a lot of him over the years, so pick a young one with good English! Medical communication can be something of a minefield. I struggle with it, and I am a doctor!

~

On Being Run Over By a Shop

AFTER A WHILE OF LIVING in this country, you start to take Thai life for granted. That which once drew inward gasps of breath no longer quickens the pulse, and items that we would initially and incredulously point out are now commonplace. But we should not lose sight of these items. They are part of what makes this country so magical.

Take the simple fact that Thailand is one of the few countries in the world where you can be run over by a shop. Yes, a shop!

In the past six months I have had several near misses by shops-in-a-hurry to get to their favourite retail stamping ground. These have included mobile kitchens selling *gai yang* (BBQ chicken), a dried squid shop and my favourite, which I christened, 'The Sticker Man' many moons ago.

They have much in common. They are motorcycle derived devices; one side is for propulsion, and the other side is for commerce. Some vendors go to great pains to display and publicise just what they are selling.

In Pattaya there is a mobile shop that sells the North-eastern delicacies. You know, the tasty morsels beloved by the Isan folk. Water beetles *(maeng da)* that look like cockroaches on steroids, strangely dissected frogs and my favourite; deep-fried scorpions. This 'retail outlet' advertises the cost of his wares, plus a 20 baht surcharge if you wish to take a photo or video, irrespective of the size of your order, or otherwise.

But I strayed from telling you about the Sticker Man. This mobile shop tops them all, in my humble shopper's opinion. This started as a vehicle to display various vinyl name stickers—Ferrari, Honda, Opel, Manchester United, Fly United, No Smoking, Marlboro, and a myriad of others. Then he added plastic windmills and signs in Thai script, which are apparently translated as 'Don't touch my girl' or 'Don't touch my car'—a sort of Thai equivalent of the Mafia musing: 'Toucha my car, I breaka you face!'

The stickers sold well and he then expanded to include blow up vinyl toys (no, not that kind! Though nothing would surprise!) that could be used as children's floaties, and as the *'pièce de résistance'*, several inflatable swans, resplendent in white with orange beaks! By now, the mobile shop is so laden down with merchandise that the driver has to peer between swans, beach rings and windmills, as well as the reams of stickers, to see his customers.

This shop will run you down very easily, since he has no vision to the left or right and forwards is only by kind courtesy of the third swan from the left lifting its wing.

However, there are even more, almost uniquely, Thai traps for the unwary motorists. The largest amongst these are the herds of loitering elephants (*chang*) that walk along poorly lit roads at night. I am sure they have all been listening to the powers that be and none are carrying the bananas to sell to tourists who never have the opportunity to see, touch or feed an elephant in their home countries.

Stopping the tourist-elephant connection is a wise move, because otherwise the visitors go into frenzies of delight, tell their friends, and produce overcrowding at the inward 'tourist visa on arrival' desk.

But again I digress. Wandering elephants are a fact of life in Thailand, for all those who do not live on Wireless Road or Ratchadamnoen Avenue, the royal passage. They are also a very homogenous shade of grey that disappears and merges with the shadows, until your headlights pick them up at the last minute. Attempting to move several tonnes of pachyderm with a Peugeot is not recommended.

I sometimes wonder if the city fathers might not do better by legislating tail lights for elephants, rather than attempting to legislate them off the suburban roads. There is even an optimistic beach south of Pattaya that declares itself rabies and elephant free. It must be pleasing to know that the local *soi* dogs and itinerant elephants can all read English!

Having mentioned dogs, I am reminded of the incredible understanding by the Thai *soi* dog of its place in the overall scheme of things. *Soi* dog knows, that as a species, it was here long before the invasion of the Toyota Corolla, so consequently the *soi,* the streets, belong to the keeper of those side streets—the *soi* dogs. This gives them the right to lie down in the middle of the road, and the Johnny-come-lately Corolla has to avoid them. *Soi* dogs do not move for motor cars. You just have to drive around sleeping canines!

In actual fact, Thai dogs are multitalented. Look at the abilities of Thai dogs to ride motorcycles! When you first arrive in Thailand, you will look with wonderment at a pooch riding side-saddle behind its owner on a 100cc step-through. Or even more amazingly, see a pet puppy sitting astride the small baby seat in front of the rider, with front paws firmly placed on the handlebars. After a while, this spectacle becomes so frequent that you do not even see it any more. It has become commonplace.

While still on motorcycles, there are so many quaint Thai factors that used to invoke interest, but again, and sadly, I and any other *farang* in Thailand no longer register them, so they have become apparently unseen. (Perhaps this is where the 'Unseen in Thailand' promotion came from?) How many people can you carry on a motorcycle? Four? Easy. Five—still easy. It's only when you get to six and above that it gets even a little squeezy!

I am waiting for an enterprising motorcycle manufacturer to advertise their new 125cc as the 'ideal transport for a family of five!'

Which brings us back to shops on motorcycles, and where we began. May you never be run over!

~

Thailand is the only place in the world where you can be run over by a shop; be it a mobile kitchen, or an over-ambitious salesman carrying his entire stock on his bike.

Phoney Thai Money

MANY PEOPLE IMAGINE THAT ASIA is the capital of the 'knock-offs', be that Crocodile T-shirts, Chanel Number 5 perfume, Rolex (Lorex) watches or the latest box-office hit movies on DVD. There is also a growing trade in fake credit cards, and some spectacular counterfeit currency.

While the more usual currency that is liable to be counterfeit is the US $100 bill, and many banks will not accept certain serial numbers of these denominations, some enterprising counterfeiters are now producing fake Thai money, and people are being duped. Since the largest denomination Thai bank note is only worth US $25, why would you bother?

However, it is not the top denomination of the 1,000 baht bill that is being reproduced, it is rare Thai coins worth millions of baht, when genuine, but a few thousand baht only when fake. But the chance of scooping up a rare bargain and making millions can sometimes be too much of a temptation.

The latest round of fakes came to the notice of world renowned numismatist Jan Olav Aamlid, who just happens to live around the corner from me. Jan had heard that some special Thai 'bullet' coins were being offered in Paris, and sold for many millions.

The coins in question were the very rare commemorative bullet coins issued on 24 May 1880, in the reign of the Thai King Rama V, in the memory of his mother Somdej Pra Dhep Sirintramat. Six denominations from two baht up to 80 baht were made, and in total only eight sets were produced. Today, three sets survive, so when the two top denominations (40 baht and 80 baht) were offered in Paris it set the coin collecting world buzzing. Being the owner of one of the three known remaining sets, Jan Olav Aamlid was not buzzing, but certainly curious.

The coins were eventually knocked down for 3.5 million baht at auction, but the would-be purchaser demanded that the authenticity be checked and the two coins were air-freighted to Thailand to be assessed by Jan Olav Aamlid.

'I was excited when I opened the box,' said Aamlid, 'but that quickly turned to disappointment when I saw that these were very poorly crafted fakes.'

Where the real 40 and 80 baht bullet coins (which are roughly spherical in shape) have designs that were engraved by craftsmen, the fakes have had the designs stamped in. There are also different sizes of the designs in the genuine article, where in the fakes, the same sized stamp has been used on both coins. I was lucky enough that Jan Olav allowed me to hold both the counterfeits and his real items. There was no getting away from it—blind Freddie could see the difference. Instead of being worth at least 3.5 million baht (around US $100,000), the lumps of silver are probably only worth around 20,000 baht as ingot silver.

Another Thai coin that has recently been the subject of the counterfeiters is the Gold *Met Kanoon* (gold jackfruit) coin. This is a gold coin shaped like a jackfruit and not a finished bullet coin. One of these was also sold in the Paris auction, and similarly was a fake.

It is believed that the counterfeit coins are actually made in Thailand and are being sold in the nation's markets, to unsuspecting tourists, or collectors with no real experience of this type of coin. The fakes then turn up in coin marketplaces overseas when the tourist attempts to cash in his holiday bonanza.

Jan Olav Aamlid also believes that there are some well-organised confidence tricksters involved, who are now looking at expanding their market to overseas auctions. So you should now add fake Thai historical coins to your list!

As a professional numismatist, Jan Olav believes that the auction houses have to be more diligent in authenticating items before offering them at auction, but this obviously did not happen at the Paris offering.

He also believes that collectors should always have their 'investment' checked by an expert or reputable dealer before spending large sums on coins that may not be quite what they are purported to be.

In the business world 'due diligence' is expected in any transaction, with the purchaser making sure that everything is as it purports to be. Unfortunately, common greed can lead to a coin collector forgetting the simple rule of *'caveat emptor'* (let the buyer beware).

Jan Olav Aamlid can be contacted by email through coin@loxinfo.co.th. And if you are holding a large spherical lump of silver with Thai designs on it, it would be well worth making the contact, before you hand over large lumps of 'real' money. The chances are that it is a 'real' fake!

~

Reinventing the Self

I WAS ONCE ASKED THE question, 'What are the pros and cons of living in Pattaya?'

My flippant reply at the time was, 'Well you've just described the population!' (If you hear this remark ascribed to anyone else, it has been stolen! It is a guaranteed original.)

While the reply was in jest, unfortunately it is not all that far from the truth. A few years ago, there were certain parts of South Pattaya that the local police were apparently ensuring were 'prostitute-free zones'. Unfortunately the boys in brown were only looking for pale skinned blonde ladies from former Iron Curtain countries.

That left a fair swag of professional maidens (oxymoron, I know) of dusky hue with dark eyes and long black hair who have been known to entertain a dalliance or two, in return for certain financial favours. It is hard to think of them all as merely enthusiastic amateurs, though I may be doing them all an injustice! But I doubt it.

The fact that many bars in Pattaya have their own occasional bedroom suites upstairs cannot just be coincidence, or down to a caring management that wishes to make sure the clients are rested before they go home. Pattaya does have its pros.

And so to cons. Unfortunately, although there are several of the dusky hued maidens with the aforementioned long black hair who are undoubtedly confidence tricksters (there are more 'sick buffaloes' in the families of Pattaya ladies than there are actual buffaloes in all of Thailand and Laos combined—sick or otherwise), but there are, I believe, many more confidence tricksters that better fit the description of Caucasian. And they don't even own one buffalo.

There have been several notorious ones, who were eventually exposed for what they were, and in most cases they were true and unrepentant 'confidence tricksters'. These were people who had made money illegally in their own countries, and came here to be 'big shots', using the misappropriated money to set themselves up in legitimate businesses.

However, eventually their past catches up with them and deportation is the best outcome that can befall them. Thai jail is the worst. For the purposes of this exercise, I do not need to elaborate and 'name names'. That has been done already by Interpol and other international police forces. And if you think deportation is a cheap ride home, think again. You stay in jail until you, or somebody else, pays for your one-way ticket out of Bangkok.

There are also what I call 'small time' cons that think Thailand in general, and Pattaya in particular, will be good places to run their scams. Fake gold, magic fluid that duplicates bank notes, or removes black ink from other currencies, bob up from time to time. Stolen traveller's cheques are becoming less and less common, as the use of international credit cards has boomed.

The new cons have card readers and other electronic trickery to get money out of (other people's) legitimate accounts. Mind you, one not-so-bright thief in Chiang Mai used a stolen credit card to buy items and then gave her address for delivery of the goods! She was promptly arrested at home the next morning.

I have also joked that there are people living in Pattaya who wrote their CV (Curriculum Vitae) on the plane coming over. Again a flippant remark, but again one that is unfortunately close to the truth. We have all met them; people who claim to be something or someone, but the claim is founded only in their own imagination. Sad.

Sad in many ways, because eventually they stumble and fall, and the house of cards collapses around them. Unfortunately, even in the so-called 'backward' Southeast Asia, after a while the subterfuge is at first questioned, and then shown to be what it was—a lie, a con, and the person has to move on.

This particularly prevalent con trick of falsely selling themselves up can be seen in the titles people will bestow upon themselves. It gets to the stage where people automatically begin to doubt the veracity of anyone with a title. And before you ask, I am a 'real' medical doctor, trained in Australia, graduated in London and with Australian postgraduate college membership.

However, I have met others in Thailand who claimed to be colleagues and were not. Or even more sad, colleagues who have been struck off their own country's medical register, but attempt to hide this fact and start again in 'fair game' Thailand.

This type of behaviour is regarded as a neurotic 'acting out' by some psychologists, and there is much of this, not only in Pattaya, but over all of Thailand itself. There is nothing fundamentally wrong with presenting yourself in a 'good' light, but there are deep seated problems when you 'make up' rather large chunks of your past life.

However, for many people, the opportunity to gild the lily is too attractive. After all, there is nobody here from your previous part of the world, say Hicksville USA, or Sleepyshire, UK. Who will find you out? The sad answer is, 'everybody'.

It has been many years since this type of confidence trick could be pulled off successfully. Even the loyal citizens of Hicksville, USA and Sleepyshire, UK can travel the world these days, and with the advent of the Internet and search engines such as Google, falsehoods are very quickly found out.

As a quick exercise, go to google.com and type in your own name. You may be amazed (or horrified) by the information that is 'out there' on you.

However, you can also meet some amazing people in Thailand. Anyone who voluntarily leaves their own society to live in an alien land is not your average suburban Mr Jones. They all have a story. They all have a past that they wished to leave behind (or escape from). The trick is guessing which it is!

~

Immigration Raids

ONE ONGOING PART OF THE life of an ex-pat in this country is getting to know your Immigration Police Department. Almost everything you want to do seems to involve this organisation.

You have a 12-month visa? Great, but you must report every 90 days to show you are still here. You want to go overseas for a holiday? Please remember to let Immigration know before you go, or otherwise you will be back to square one when you return. Mention the word 'immigration' and many *farang*s turn pale (or even paler than usual).

The ex-pat hangout bars are always hotbeds of gossip about the Immigration Police and its raids—Police rushing in with cameras blazing to catch the miscreant immigrant on a tourist visa found working illegally. Newspapers are full of ex-pats who have overstayed their visas and are now residing at the Immigration 'hotel' until someone coughs up the money for the one-way air ticket from Bangkok to wherever-the-hell-they-came-from.

Having been witness to a couple of Immigration Police raids, I have to say that it isn't quite the way you hear it in the bar. Nor is Thailand the only country in the world to carry out immigration raids. Read on!

One day I was sitting in a rather upmarket Kashmiri restaurant in Pattaya that had just opened. Dark faces were everywhere, Kashmiri musicians serenaded the diners and Kashmiri cooks were looking to see whether the customers were enjoying their food.

I noticed three very casually dressed Thai men come in and sat at a table. Waving the waitress away, they refused the menu, but then one pulled out a small handycam and proceeded to film the musicians, the waiters, the Maitre d' and anyone else who looked non-Thai. The manager was called over, 'sotto voce' mutterings took place, and slowly the Kashmiris filed outside. My meal order was cancelled, as they no longer had a chef! Apologies all round, and that was raid number 1.

Raid number 2 took place in Australia, that land of milk and honey, koala bears (yes, I know they are really marsupials and not bears) and the world's last bastion of 'mateship' and fair play. I was the owner of a Thai restaurant in Brisbane Australia, called Thai Tasty. It was an authentic Thai restaurant, with a Thai cook (*Bong*), Thai cashiers, Thai waitresses and Thai kitchen hands, but the cook, who lived close to Ayutthaya and who had not forgotten or forgiven, selected a Burmese cleaner!

Bong was a great cook who worked seven days. In fact, when I hired him, that was his stipulation—he had to work seven days or he didn't want the job! He was paid accordingly, of course. On his birthday he took half the day off. When he applied he showed me his all-important Tax File number that all employees in Australia must have, and his taxes were deducted each week.

Bong had been with me about two and a half years when we received a visit from the Federal Police. That visit was unannounced and heralded by three burly policemen waving handguns, bursting in through the front of the restaurant, whilst another, complete with another loaded weapon, came up the rear stairs and in through the back door. There in the kitchen they surrounded my cook, who was armed with a lethal soup ladle. With shouts that he was an illegal immigrant, he was frogmarched into the waiting police vehicle and driven off!

My remaining staff were terrified, but called me, and I began to try to make some sense of all this. Was my cook the Burmese drug overlord Khun Sa or what?

I managed to find the Federal Police officer in charge, who informed me that *Bong* had entered Australia on a visitor's visa and had overstayed its provisions by four years. Heinous crime!

I went into their office to discuss what was going to happen next. I appealed to their better natures that the only crime *Bong* had committed was that he had the wrong piece of paper; a visitor's visa instead of a work visa. He had paid tax, had a tax file number and was an outstanding employee, but that apparently didn't matter.

I asked how they came to single out my cook, but the Federal Police came over coy about that, and said they were still to interrogate *Bong*, as they were waiting for the official interpreter, a Thai lady by the name of *Metinee*. Of course *Bong*, who could actually speak very good English, would not say a word either.

The police sat back triumphantly, with the 'criminal' apprehended, and I was asked to return after the interpreter had arrived. What the Feds did not realise was that their official interpreter also worked as one of my kitchen hands! She soon rang me to tell me what had happened. My satay cook, with some pressing gambling debts, had informed the Federal Police to get the bounty that the Australian Immigration Police offered for information leading to the arrest of illegal immigrants.

I returned and informed the senior policeman that I knew just how they had discovered my cook's visa was wrong, and how I thought it was all very underhand, and 'un-Australian'.

A bargain was struck. They would hold *Bong* overnight, providing I could get him a one-way plane ticket out of Australia for the next day. Otherwise he would be charged, put in prison for six weeks and then found guilty and deported.

I got the plane ticket, and *Bong* departed. My satay cook was fired. The other Thai restaurants sent me cooks on rotation to keep my restaurant going till I could get a permanent replacement, a selfless act that still leaves me in awe of Thai national pride.

But I have not forgotten how the Immigration Police worked down-under, how they used the bounty system, and how they needed drawn revolvers to apprehend a mild mannered Thai cook.

Perhaps the raids here aren't so bad after all!

PS. I have changed the names to protect the guilty!

~

On Getting a Bank Loan

As a farang in Thailand, it is difficult to open a bank account. Certain residency-style visas are needed and even if you are successful, you will find the interest rate you get on your savings bank account is less than for those account holders who are native born. In a country which has in its charter that there shall be no discrimination through race, someone forgot to tell the banks!

However, I do have bank accounts in different banks, and have had so for many years, so I was not at all apprehensive on going to my main bank to ask for a house loan. Or rather 'houses' loan. Let me explain.

My wife had found this new housing estate with inexpensive houses, and managed to secure the last one for us by putting down a holding deposit before we went overseas on a holiday. On our return she withdrew the necessary remainder of the deposit and went to see the sales office lady. There in the line in front of her was a woman who was supposed to be doing the same, but had a tale of woe, unable to go through with the purchase. Since this house was directly opposite 'our' house, my wife made the split second decision and slapped a holding deposit on that house too.

We had left on our holiday with nothing and within one week of our return we were negotiating on two houses! Had I just become a property tycoon? And all for two times 50,000 baht deposits!

However, we would need a bank loan for the rest, but my beloved had already made inquiries and the repayments were well within our reach on our combined salaries, which without being churlish, really meant mine!

We made an appointment to see the Loans Officer at my bank and I spent an evening jotting down our outgoings and incomings, expected rentals from the second house—a complete business plan that should satisfy any bean counter.

So it was with a confident air that we approached the bank officer. I began by asking whether my age was going to be a problem for the bank. I was assured that this was no problem, because I had a permanent job, had a work permit and was well known. We smiled, and so did he, in that wonderful Thai way.

I continued, explaining why we wanted two houses on this loan, and how the second house would pay off its own mortgage and so would not be a financial drain on our resources. The smile faded.

'*Mai dai*,' (cannot) was the first response from our friendly loans officer.

'Why *mai da*'?' I asked.

'Because this would need a business loan.'

'I see, so what about two loans then, one for each house?' I asked while smiling pleasantly, displaying my entire dental records to anyone in a bank uniform, hovering around us.

'*Mai dai*. Can only loan for one house.'

At this stage my wife began an exchange in Thai and after five minutes '*mai dai*' turned into '*Dai, dai*' with lots of head nodding.

'How did you manage to bring him around?' I asked.

'It was easy, I just told him the second house was for Mama and Papa!'

However, we had not overcome the problem of having two houses on the one bank loan, but the Loan Arranger himself came up with the answer.

'Are the houses less than 100 metres apart?' After the affirmative answer, he then continued, 'OK. OK. Then we call them one house!'

So in no time at all we had gone from two three bedroom houses with one for rent, which could not be done, to two three bedroom houses with one for Mama and Papa and then to one six bedroom house which could be done (even though they were on opposite sides of the street)!

In this somewhat bizarre scenario we then sat down to see what paperwork we would need. This is not a simple procedure, let me assure you. It is not enough to bring in a copy of your employment contract. You also have to bring in the salary slip you get each month, A copy of the bank statements for the past six months and the taxation receipt for the salary. Now photocopy each one twice and then sign each page. Ah yes, you're married, so photocopy the marriage license twice and both of you have to sign them.

Then there are even more papers to sign, but since this is Thailand and official documents have to be in Thai, I have no idea what I was expected to sign. The brain was numb by then (and my backside), and I was fighting writer's cramp. I just smiled and signed, smiled and signed and smiled and signed! The Loan Arranger also smiled, clipped everything together and told us he would ring and let us know how it was going.

Over the next few weeks, he would ring and get us in to sign more documents, all of which were in Thai, and all of which were equally indecipherable.

After two months, I was beginning to get just a tad annoyed. I took to ringing him each week, to be fobbed off as usual, or even worse, he would revert to his native Thai, in which I have the ability to order food and find toilets and not much else. Customer satisfaction was not at an all-time high.

After three months I was rung by head office, to be told that our application for the six bedroom house had been rejected.

'Could you please tell me why?' I asked.

'Oh, sorry sir, but you are too old,' was the reply.

'But your Loans Officer told me that my age was not a problem.'

'Sorry sir, but he should not have said that.'

I could see I had gone the full circle. 'What do I do now?' I asked.

'No problem, sir. Just go to two other banks and apply for one house loan in each.'

I resigned myself to this, and comforted myself with the fact that now I knew a little bit more about the Thai banking system.

So my wife and I began the loan application roundabout again. Several forests were chopped down to get us enough photocopies for two loan applications, and we began the waiting game all over again.

Finally the loan for the 'rental' house came through, and my wife and I only have to live for the next 30 years and it will be all ours. However, at least the mortgage repayments are less than the projected rental income. It should pay itself off. Our children will be pleased.

But we still had not got the loan for the house we wanted to live in. This second bank decided after two months that we needed a guarantor. Fortunately, I do have some friends not as impecunious as myself, and a chap with a platinum Amex card stepped up to the plate to be our man. We thanked him and sat back expectantly. However, nothing in Thailand is that easy, I should have known by now.

There was the small matter of the military coup d'etat. A bank holiday was called the day after the coup. The day we were supposed to visit the bank. We called the next day, but nobody was available to tell us how the application had gone. Or the next day. Or the next.

Finally after one week we were told that our platinum Amex cardholder friend was not good enough. From now on, the new bank guidelines were that all guarantors have to be Thai nationals. I began to feel racially discriminated against again. As well as being back to square one.

Of course, our own rented house contract has now ended, so if you see a tent on the footpath outside one of the major banks in Thailand, spare a thought for the occupants. It is probably us waiting for a bank loan!

~

The Prince and I

THERE WAS A FILM YEARS ago, *The King and I*, starring Yul Brynner, which was an enormously successful movie, loosely based on the book *Anna and the King of Siam*, written by Anna Leonowens. My version I have called 'The Prince and I' but the difference between mine and hers is that mine is factual!

I used to do a weekly feature for the *Pattaya Mail* newspaper, called 'Local Personality' and there was an amazingly similar thread that ran through the profiles. Those who had chosen Thailand in which to live, as opposed to those who had been sent here by their employers, had all felt some strange affinity to the country when they first visited.

For myself, it was the same. When I first landed I got out of the aircraft at the old Don Muang International Airport, stood on the tarmac waiting for the bus to the terminal, and turned to my mates and said, 'I'm home!' I had no idea why I felt like that, but I did. My mates put it down to too many Singha beers on the flight, a phenomenon which is not unheard of, I have to admit.

However, my love affair with the kingdom of Thailand stretched back even further than that. Back to the time when I was a small boy in short trousers, freezing my knees off in Scotland. By the time I had reached 10 years of age, I was infatuated with motorcars. For years, on my way home, I would walk into car sales showrooms and cadge the brochures which I would cut up and stick in scrapbooks. Yes, I remember the brand new 1953 Morris Oxford, which incidentally is still made today, but in India and called the Hindustan Ambassador! Trivia that should have been forgotten. Or rather, a car that should have been forgotten!

My next door neighbour had a motorcycle and I would sit on a pillow strapped to the mudguard, and he would take me to the motor racing meetings at Charterhall, outside Duns. There I saw drivers such as the future world champions Jimmy Clark and Jackie Stewart, and others like (now Sir) Stirling Moss.

My infatuation turned into obsession. I knew I had to go motor racing, though it took me many years before I could afford to get behind the wheel in anger. In the meantime, I devoured and collected anything I could find about motor racing and racing drivers.

I collected a photograph of British driver Mike Hawthorn (who became world champion in 1958 and was killed on the road a few months later), which was part of a window display for Craven A cigarettes in the local tobacconist's window. Eventually he gave it to me, just to stop me coming in every day and begging for it. I mounted it on my bedroom wall.

I also collected a painting of a blue and yellow ERA (English Racing Automobiles) which had been built in 1936. This was also mounted on my bedroom wall. This car was a light blue colour with a yellow chassis and yellow wheels. These were the newly assigned racing colours for the country then called Siam, and now called Thailand.

The car had been called Hanuman by its owner, who was the Siamese Prince Chula Chakrabongse, who ran a racing team based in the UK, called White Mouse Racing. His driver was Prince Birabongse Bhanutej Bhanubandh, who was also a member of Siam's royal family and was a grandson of King Mongkut (of *Anna and the King of Siam*). He was known as Prince Bira, mainly because Birabongse Bhanutej Bhanubandh was far too much of a mouthful for the British motor racing public.

When my family emigrated to Australia when I was 14, the painting of Prince Bira's Hanuman came with me, and was mounted on my new bedroom wall Down Under.

It was to be many years later, after my first trip to Thailand, that I became aware of the Ramakien, the wonderful folklore relating to Prince Rama, and of his faithful monkey god companion called Hanuman. The image of the blue and yellow ERA now had historical significance as well!

But it didn't end there. From 1975, I used to come to Thailand every year on holidays, and each year the feeling of being 'home' got stronger. I knew that one day I would come to Thailand to live permanently, and presumed that I would be living in Bangkok.

However each year, as I saw the traffic jams getting worse, I began to think of being further afield. Pattaya was one of those proposed destinations, as was Phuket and Chiang Mai. I visited them all, but Pattaya had the wild card. Pattaya had a motor racing circuit on its outskirts. It was called the Prince Bira International Circuit.

Now another contact had been made in Thailand, and that was with Dr Prachin Eamlumnow, the owner of Grand Prix International, who also controlled the Bira International Circuit. When I told him in 1997 that I was coming to Thailand to live permanently, I was picked up at the airport and taken to his office. We spoke about Prince Bira, and it turned out that he was a fan of the late prince as well. We had a common bond.

One hour later I emerged as the 'International Consultant' for the Bira International Circuit! The die had been cast. I visited the circuit and stood before the bust of Prince Bira at the shrine near the main gate. I thanked him. This was my destiny!

But it does not end there. Early in the new millennium I was told about an old blue racing car seen for sale in London. It had yellow wheels and a white mouse on the rear vision mirrors! Team White Mouse! Was this Prince Bira's Hanuman?

I was given a London telephone number and I rang, my heart beating with excitement. Could I bring Hanuman to Thailand? In my mind's eye, I could see the old race car on display at the circuit.

The call confirmed that unfortunately it wasn't Hanuman, but was another of the Siamese Prince's ERAs, called Remus. This car was even more famous than Hanuman and was for sale. Only one problem. The owner wanted the equivalent of 47 million baht. That was 47 million problems!

I tried to muster a consortium to bring this legendary car to Thailand. After all, Prince Bira was the first Thai international sportsman of world standard, long before the snooker playing James Wattana, or the latter day tennis playing Paradorn. Prince Bira had won the BRDC Gold Star for three years in a row; 1936, 1937 and 1938. That was the equivalent of today's F1 championship.

However, in post economic crash Thailand it was not possible for this *farang* to know how to get such an astronomical sum together. I felt I had let down Prince Bira, and the country I now called home. I still hope that one day I can get Hanuman to live out its days in Thailand, and if I could ever drive it around the Prince Bira Circuit, that would be the high point of my own racing career.

I still continue to dream!

~

'Electric Bisikun'—my faithful chariot for the charity cycle around Pattaya. When the electric engine faltered, so did I.

The Tour de Pattaya

PATTAYA HAS A LONG TRADITION of charity bike rides. Well at least five years anyway, (in Pattaya where businesses can close before their official 'grand opening', five years really is aeons).

This particular bike ride is part of the annual Jesters Care for Kids charity drive, and regularly brings in over 200,000 baht towards the grand total, which this year topped 4 million baht.

However, I too have a long tradition, unfortunately intertwined with vanity and perversity, and since you asked, it is a lifelong inability to turn down a challenge. You can see the scene already? A 50-kilometre bike ride and a challenge to take part. And you can't say, 'No!'

How childish, some may think, but look from my side for a moment. You are 60-something years of age and some sly grinning young whippersnapper invites you to do the 50 kilometres, expecting the excuses from someone who does not wish to admit to aging in any way. Well, he got no excuses from me. 'Great idea,' was my rejoinder, but said with an even greater sly grin.

You see, I have always believed in the maxim that Age, Experience and Animal Cunning will beat Youth and Enthusiasm any day. It was time to start exhibiting some and playing a few of the aces I have secreted up my sleeve over the years for use in emergencies. Ace One was a friend in Bangkok, Paul Markham, whose company (EcoBrand) made electric bicycles. Paul was receptive to my plan, and an EcoBrand sports-racer was delivered, complete with battery and charger.

This thing looked great, and on first glance you could miss the fact that the central down-tube was actually a ruddy great battery. I electro-pedalled home to show my good lady, who immediately named it, 'The Electric Bisikun' and the name stuck.

I was a little worried whether Electric Bisikun would do the whole 50 clicks, but Paul said that as long as I used a bit of pedal power, it would make it. Reassured, I lined up with the other 100 or so riders and the charity ride was on.

Mixing it with the others, I just kept pace with those on leg-power, but when we came to the first hill, lekky-power showed its inherent advantage. As they grunted and sweated, climbing out of their saddles, they were passed by this grey haired gent who was just sitting there, pedalling steadily past them.

Back on the flat, they came up again, with some feeling that something about this entry wasn't quite kosher. 'What's the big thing in the centre with Eco written on it?'

'Uh that,' I replied, 'That's an ozone generator, and as I pedal it releases ozone to seal the hole in the ozone layer.'

Some even fell for it (didn't you, Sooz), but others began to twig.

'That's against the rules,' was exclaimed, but when I pointed out that this was a charity ride, not a race, and as I was raising money for kids, what did it matter that I was using modern technology? After all, the aces were using bikes with plenty of techno improvements over the standard two wheeled devices—carbon-fibre forks, kevlar rims and other such space age materials to end up with 12 kg bikes.

Electric Bisikun covered the 50 kilometeres in a little over two hours and I received my certificate, and hung it on the wall; a tangible example of Age, Experience and the aforementioned Animal Cunning!

The following year I was asked again by the organisers to enter, and bring my lekky bike, as it had generated its own team of fans. It was time for another phone call, and a new model, complete with lights and sirens, was delivered.

This time I was brimful of confidence, and with lights flashing and sirens going, would speed past the others on the uphill ranges. Pride comes before a fall, they say. I was about to take my tumble.

By halfway round the course, I noticed the voltmeter was registering a very strong zero. Suddenly the uphill sections were agony. Lekky Bisikuns are heavy buggers—the battery alone is twice as heavy as some bikes. The ride finished in agony, however, it was still again just over two hours, and the second certificate was hung with the first.

So to this year. 'Paul, I need a bike and two batteries!' (See what Experience can do for you?) Paul delivered bisikun with the extra battery the day before the event. One battery was given to my mate Kurt who was marshalling at the 30k marker. I was ready!

There's another saying about the best-laid plans of mice and men going astray. Now who has ever heard of mice plans? By kilometre 20 I was in trouble. The rear brake was adjusted too tightly and my battery was fighting not only the gradients, but dragging brakes **as** well. And I had no tools on board!

A friendly water-stop person phoned ahead to Kurt, and a marshal brought the second battery back to the powerless bicycle. By this stage, everyone bar children on tricycles had passed me, and when I eventually got to the next water stop, the marshals had all gone home! There wasn't a note to say, 'Got tired of waiting, help yourself,' but I got the hidden message anyway.

I continued, but the dragging brake was damaging battery number two, and the 61-year-old rider was also knackered by this stage. At 30 kilometres I accepted the offer of a lift and Electric Bisikun and two flat batteries were consigned to the back of a pickup.

Ignominy! But wait till next year, I said to myself! 'Paul, I want a Tour de France racer and three batteries, and a tool kit,' would be my next request.

Age, Experience and Animal Cunning would triumph. Wait and see.

(Footnote: After that year the bike ride was cancelled, so I'll never know if I could make the 50k again!)

~

Water Into Wine

FOR MANY YEARS, I HAVE been able to turn wine into water, but it took a spell in hospital to show me how to turn water into wine. Interested? It came about after I spent some time in my hospital, but not in my usual role of a white coat wearing consultant, but rather in the role of a blue-pyjama'd patient. One that I do not take kindly to.

It began a few months ago. I noticed I was getting a trifle puffed walking from the car park to my office. I was also very tired at night, but just put it down to getting older. In fact, it was becoming a bit of a struggle getting about, but ah well, maybe that's what happens when you race past 60.

The next symptom was my urine getting darker, but I chose to ignore that. You see, there are two types of doctors, in my experience. The first one rushes to the medical cupboard at the first sign of a cough or sniffle, and takes something to make sure the condition does not progress. The second type studiously ignores all signs of illness as being personal weakness and not to be pandered to. After all, medicos just get better. I belong to the latter group.

So here I was, getting more and more tired, until one day I noticed that my pee was now the colour of a full-bodied claret. In wine appreciation terminology it might have been scored as, 'a deep red colour with an ammoniacal nose and a nitrate odour leaving an objectionable aftertaste which does not seem to improve with aeration.'

At that stage I knew I could ignore this no longer, but consulted one of my colleagues, looking for reassurance that this was just a passing (water) phase. He took one look at the claret urine and rejecting my suggestion of two wine glasses and a platter of cheese, sent me off for some tests. An anxious 30 minutes followed while we waited for the results. (It is salient to note that in Australia the wait would have been anything up to a couple of days, and in the UK it would have been a couple of weeks.)

The results were not good. In fact the results were so bad that I had to exchange the white coat for the aforementioned blue pyjamas immediately and was confined to bed. My pee had more red blood cells than urine electrolytes. My blood haemoglobin count was down to 50% of where it should have been. In other words, I was in deep doggy doo, to use a non-clinical term. Put simply, I was peeing my lifeblood away, which was reducing the oxygen carrying capacity of the circulating blood to half. No wonder I was getting puffed!

Now to fully diagnose what is going on in the kidneys requires us medicos to carry out a fun procedure called a 'kidney biopsy'. This is done with the patient conscious, as you have to follow some commands, while you lie face down and helpless on a folded up towel to push your kidneys into your back. Once suitably positioned, the doctor carrying out the biopsy inserts a sampling instrument through your back, akin to a piece of railway line with a hole down the middle, and transfixes the kidney and withdraws a core sample, similar to drilling for oil in the ocean bed. This is such a fun procedure, that they do this several times, to make sure they have enough core samples!

Biopsies over, you are then forced to lie on your back, on a house brick (well that's what it feels like), for six hours to put pressure on the kidney to stop the bleeding. On the third day, some big gun treatment was wheeled out. Enough large doses of steroids to make me ready for the Tour de France or even *Terminator 5*. The word 'terminator' was actually not too far-fetched. This was serious doggy doo.

Word of the seriousness got out, and that evening, my friend Pascal Schnyder from Casa Pascal restaurant sent up three service personnel bearing a large platter of salmon and cheese with all the trimmings, all the linen and cutlery, an ice bucket and a well chilled bottle of champagne and two flutes. My wife tentatively asked whether my doctor would agree to the champagne, but

I told her that I was not asking my treating doctor, I was asking Dr Iain Corness, and he said the thick end of half a bottle would be fine.

After all, being miserable and sick is as excellent a reason as I can think of, and one more than Madam Lilly Bollinger, of the Bollinger brand of champagnes, has been credited with. (For followers of the lady, it is reputed that she said, 'I drink champagne when I'm happy and when I'm sad. Sometimes I drink it when I'm alone. When I have company I consider it obligatory. I trifle with it if I'm not hungry and drink it when I am. Otherwise I never touch it—unless I'm thirsty.')

The next morning I staggered out to pee in the always waiting bottle. (Have you noticed that it is almost impossible to pee when lying down? I certainly can't do it, and I'm a male with the necessary plumbing equipment! Goodness knows what women do in these circumstances?) Returning to the bottle in hand, I couldn't believe my eyes. I was peeing champagne! Forget about the alchemists turning base metals into gold, I had my own champagne factory. Well that's what it looked like anyway, even if the nose didn't correspond. But it was classic yellow straw colour, signalling the end of the water into wine miracle.

Of course my doctor was churlish enough to claim the success with the steroids, but Pascal and I knew the real reason. (And Lilly Bollinger eat your heart out, it was an Australian champagne, or Methode Champenoise if you want to be really pedantic.)

Now there will be those of you who will doubt this story, but let me assure you that every bit of it is true. And if you don't believe me, I can send you a bottle of the last vintage!

~

Two Tuesdays in the One House

ANYONE WHO HAS BEEN IN Thailand for more than three weeks will know that Thai people are very superstitious. Great stock is placed upon spirits, magic, omens and the like.

Every Thai woman will consult a fortune teller at some stage in their lives, particularly when advice is needed regarding affairs of the heart. It is all very fine to swamp your lady with red roses, but if the fortune teller says that her true partner is two metres tall, then you, at a mere 1.80m, can stop wasting your money on roses. The oracle has spoken.

The superstitions are so numerous, the mind boggles at just how the average Thai manages to remember them all.

Have you ever tried to get your hair cut on a Wednesday? The barbershops are shut, because it is considered bad luck to have your tonsorial splendour attacked on that day. This has more adherents than the old fish on Fridays Catholic routine.

There are also days when you should not cut your nails, but nobody has told me what happens if you are a daily nail nibbler. One day I will be appraised, after something suitably dreadful has happened.

The Adherence to Superstition Clause in the marriage contract really came to the fore last month, as the day for the birth of our second child approached. Since it was going to be a Caesarean section, my wife was told to pick the day that was most auspicious. Friday, 9 September, (the 9th month) was proposed by the obstetrician. Nine is a lucky number it appears, and the 9/9 would be doubly lucky.

So 9 September almost got the nod, but for one small problem—my wife was born on a Saturday and Saturdays and Fridays don't get on, I was told. Back to the drawing board, or should I say the geomancy tables.

My wife would sit up every night, studying the tables, counting the numbers put forward by the numerologists and probably doing incantations, but since I had by then fallen asleep, I was blissfully ignorant of any practices which might have involved chicken's entrails or magnetic pig's trotters aligned with the moon.

As the fateful week approached we looked as if we had a date—6 September, which was a Tuesday, but there was a big problem looming. Our first child was also born on a Tuesday, and two Tuesdays in the one house was considered far from serendipitous.

My wife, who really is a very practical soul, despite the fortune tellers, then decided that perhaps my birthday should be involved in the equation. There was only one problem—I had no earthly idea which day of the week I had made my entry, centre stage.

Referral to Mr Google was needed, who supplied a well out of date calendar, which showed that I too was born on a Tuesday. Smiles all round, as apparently three Tuesdays under the one roof are fine. The logic of all this escapes me, but then what have superstition and logic got in common? Not much, is the logical answer. (What's logic? is the superstitious answer).

With relief, I said that I would let the obstetrician know, so that she could organise her schedule too. 'Not yet,' was the rejoinder from the heavily pregnant one. 'We have to find the best time.'

I noted the use of 'we'; the royal plural, intimating that in some way I was involved in all of these calculations. However, since I had saved the Tuesday of the week, I supposed I could also be involved in the timing. I wracked my brains for my time of birth and remembered my mother saying, 'Some time at night,' which wasn't all that helpful.

So, back to the books and after much calculation, 7pm was pronounced the ideal time. This was imparted to the long suffering obstetrician, who sank the horologists by saying that it would have to be 4pm as she wanted the neonatologists to be on hand, and they went home at 5pm.

With reluctance, I imparted the news to my wife, realising that if anything goes wrong with this child over the next 20 years, I will be considered culpable, for having ruined the clocks. Fortunately, we obviously had enough merit points in the Bank of Superstition, that this small setback could be overcome, and the new baby would not be blighted for ever and a day.

But it does not end there, gentle reader. There is the weighty problem in choosing a name. Just coming up with 'Egbert sounds nice' is definitely not acceptable. The numerologists were called in again and the list of proposed names was subjected to scrutiny, but finally we had the name for a boy. On Tuesday, 6 September at 3.30pm, as my wife was being wheeled to theatre, I suddenly remembered that we did not have a name for a girl.

'We'll worry about that later,' said the pregnant to bursting one, who was hoping for a boy and so was not going to waste valuable time at the numerologists for a name that would not be needed.

So, at 4.39pm, Evan Corness was brought into the world, and at 4.2 kg and 57 cm long a chainsaw was almost needed in the operating theatre, but after a suitably large incision was made, he practically climbed out by himself!

My wife smiled triumphantly. After all, she knew it was going to be a boy, as the tarot card lady had predicted it, and all the omens were correct. So let us hope that young Evan does not give us too many sleepless nights. If he does, it will probably be because he was born two hours and 21 minutes early. Atheists like me cannot win under these circumstances.

~

Loy Krathong

THERE ARE TWO MAJOR THAI festivals; *Songkran*, which you dress down for, covered elsewhere in this book, and *Loy Krathong*, that you dress up for. By the afternoon of *Loy Krathong*, the streets of Thailand are just thronged with the most beautiful girls, in classical Thai costumes, and no male could be anything but impressed. The Land of Smiles becomes the Land of Beautiful Women.

The history of this festival goes back more than 700 years and is an example of Thai pragmatism. By the way, after the Burmese sacked the old capital Ayutthaya, all records were destroyed, but King Mongkut (Rama IV), in 1863, pieced together the legend, so that you and I can understand *Loy Krathong*.

In another typical Thai way, you can ask most of the beautiful girls what it is all about, and they will show that they do not know their own history. Shame really.

Returning to the legend, in the reign of Phra Ruang in the dynasty of the Sukhothai era there was a famous

Brahmin priest who had a very beautiful young daughter called Nang Noppamas. She was well-skilled in many arts and sciences, and was to be an ideal wife for the King Lithai. So they were married, and even though Nang Noppamas had married a Buddhist King, she herself followed the Brahmin tradition of her family.

In those days, it was a Brahmin tradition that one prepared suitable offerings for the spirit of the river. This would make it possible to have absolution of one's sins, similar in many ways to the principle behind the confessional in Catholicism.

Nang Noppamas had secretly prepared this small boat-like structure, called a 'krathong', made of banana leaves. She then loaded it with paddy husks to make it float in stable equilibrium. She stitched strips of plantain leaves together, and pinned them around the edge of the little boat by way of ornament. Over the ballast she spread smooth clean plantain leaves, and on this green leafy deck she placed a little cargo of betel nut, betel leaf, parched rice, and sweet scented flowers. She took several fresh fruits of a fleshy character, such as the papaya and the pumpkin, and deftly carved them into representations of fruits, flowers, and animals, and piled them up in a conical arrangement in the centre.

The artificial flowers she stained with the juices of other plants to make them resemble real blossoms. Here and there she fastened one of her own sketches or paintings, and finally finished the work by adorning it with storied umbrellas of paper, tiny flags, toy implements, tapers, and scented incense sticks. This first *krathong* captured the minds of everyone, with its intricacies and beauty, and this was the beginning of what was to become an annual ceremony.

King Lithai realised that this was a Brahmin celebration that his wife was celebrating, but rather than have division in the community, he decreed that it would also be a Buddhist celebration, and dedicated the *krathongs* to the Lord Buddha.

Following regularisation, the townspeople began to make their own *krathongs* and the ceremony was born. The King decreed that it should be an annual event in honour of the wise and beautiful Nang Noppamas. It was he who called it '*Loy Krathong*', where '*loy*' means to send adrift, and '*krathong*' means a little basket-like boat.

The ceremony has now existed for 700 years, and is celebrated all over Thailand, though like all things, has changed with time. Today the three incense sticks represent the Buddha, the Dharma (teaching) and the Sangha (community of monks and Buddhism practitioners) and people often put some hair or nail clippings in the *krathong*, along with some coins, and float it away, to carry away their cares and woes.

With the advent of the Chinese influence you get the fireworks, and of course there are the beauty pageants to find today's Nang Noppamas, which explains the surfeit of gorgeous women on the streets, all rushing home from the beauty salons.

My wife and I celebrate this event each year, and have done since the days we were beginning to become serious about each other. *Loy Krathong* is best celebrated with one's partner, and falls on the full moon in November.

Being close to the beach, we dress up and then go to the shoreline. Rather than make a *krathong* ourselves, Beach Road is packed with *krathong* sellers with little tables to display their wares, and some of the items are just spectacular.

Having selected 'our' *krathong* we then wade out to sea, light its candle and incense sticks, add some strands of hair (this is getting increasingly difficult for me, as there is precious little left), some nail clippings and a few baht in coins. Then hand in hand we watch it float out into the Gulf of Siam. What a wonderful way to commune with one's partner!

However, it isn't quite that romantic, even though it is a beautiful sight as all the *krathong*s leave the shore. As you look out to sea, there just beyond the first line of small breakers are some dark spherical shapes, descending upon the *krathong*s. These are all the local lads, silently swimming, who systematically empty the *krathong*s of their cargo; presumably the money, leaving my toe nails and hair behind! Ah well, if it takes a few baht to gain absolution, one shouldn't begrudge the young lads for capitalising on my sins.

We then sit back on two deckchairs, have a drink to celebrate in *farang* style, and watch the '*kom loys*' floating up into the sky. These are a primitive hot-air balloon, with a paraffin candle suspended underneath to fill the balloon, which is made of woven plastic threads.

I did say things had changed over the years since Nang Noppamas, didn't I?

Scurrying across the beach are the *kom loy* sellers and the firework peddlers. Of course, the police decree each year that selling fireworks is banned, but leave everyone alone to enjoy the evening. There is never a policeman to be seen. Clever policemen!

The next morning, the tide will have returned the remains of the *krathong*s to the shore, but by noon, the street sweepers and the beach concessionaires have carried away the debris, the traditional dresses have been returned to the costume hire outlets, and we wait another 12 months for the next *Loy Krathong*. And perhaps ponder on Nang Noppamas and Thai practicality. Something that makes living here just that little bit more magical.

~

The Good Time Girls

I WOULD IMAGINE THAT EVERY red-blooded male who reads this book would feel cheated if I didn't include something about the local ladies, those inhabitants of Pattaya that our Agony Aunt Hillary (of the English language weekly the *Pattaya Mail*) calls the 'good time girls'.

However, it should not be thought that these are a Pattaya exclusive, as they are also found in Bangkok, Samui, Phuket and anywhere that tourists will congregate in large enough numbers. Just like in London, Amsterdam, New York or Berlin (or anywhere in the world, for that matter).

For my money (or yours, as these are 'professional' ladies, not enthusiastic amateurs), these girls are offering a service with a smile, and undoubtedly give some of the likely lads an experience they would not get at home.

However, what many of the likely lads forget, or do not understand, is that these are not only Good Time Girls, but are also 'Short Time' girls. These are not ladies waiting to fall in love with Mr Right, or even Mr Wright. These are ladies looking to view the contents of the Wright wallet. As the iconic Ms Hillary writes: 'You don't go to a hardware shop if you want to buy cheese!'

But still they arrive here in droves looking for 100gm of cheddar in all the wrong places. And there are plenty of those. They open around 4pm and close around 4am, or whenever there are no more punters that evening.

But over they come, like lemmings going over the cliff. Head over heels in love. Sorry, that should be 'Love' with a capital L. The sweet little brown creature, who has 'only work bar this week,' and has never been with a *farang* before, will happily go with him and blow more than his socks off. Just as she did last week, the week before and the months before with a never-ending stream of *farang* 'boyfriends'.

After their three week love-fest the lemmings return to Manchester or Detroit or Melbourne and rush to their computers to email this incredible woman, their future life partner. And back will come a beautiful email indicating just how much they miss him too, how they think they are in love as well and please come back soon.

So isn't it real? Sad thing is, of course, it is not real. For one thing, for most of the Good Time Girls, their

English language skills give out after, 'Hello sexy man. Sit down please. Buy me cola. I love you too mut.'

But this barely bilingual goddess is suddenly able to put together well-written emails full of proclamations of love that would put Emily Dickinson to shame. How can this be?

Simple; there is a book, of which every bar has at least one copy, with letters to be written to smitten swains from overseas. This book makes interesting reading, including the sad news of the brother's motorcycle accident and the hospital fees, and even bulletins on the health of the family buffalo (a very illness-prone beast if ever I heard of one). There are several heart-wrenching letters on how the money that Tom, Dick or Harry has given her on leaving has run out, and she will unfortunately have to go back to working in the bar. Unless of course, Tom, Dick or Harry could send her just a few baht regularly each month—then she could go back to the village and look after Mumma, who is currently looking after the one-legged brother (they couldn't afford the operation) and the sick buffalo.

The trap has been made, and now it will be sprung. Tom, Dick or Harry will rescue his maiden in distress and at least 30,000 baht a month will appear in her bank account. But it is not Tom, Dick or Harry—it is Tom, Dick and Harry; Tom from the US, Dick from Australia and Harry from Belgium. That's three times 30,000 baht every month. 90,000 baht a month is better than most Thai people will earn in 12 months. So who is the poor little exploited person here? Not our Good Time

Girl! Tom, Dick and Harry have just been sexploited, to coin a phrase.

With the permission of the *Pattaya Mail* and Ms Hillary, here are a few excerpts from letters from those who have made the mistake of confusing a 'good time' with a 'long time'.

Dear Hillary,

Do these men who claim to have lost money on motorcycles, cars, houses, gold chains, injured brothers and terminally ill buffaloes, really exist? Every week there seems to be another tale of woe. Do they never learn from reading about the others who went before them? Surely there are not that many? Tell me that you make those letters up each week?
- Disbelieving Dennis.

Dear Disbelieving Dennis,

The sad fact is, my disbelieving Petal, that these people do exist. They come over in swarms every year, with the sick buffaloes lining up in the stalls, waiting for financial fodder. Why don't they learn by reading what has gone before? Because I think they can't read.

★

Dear Hillary,

Why is there so much in your Agony Aunt column about love-sick, spurned and hopeless men? Don't they understand that all of life is a lottery and there's only a few winning tickets. When you don't win this one then you line up again for the next lottery—after all there's plenty of lotteries and plenty of tickets! I buy a new lottery ticket every week and I'm enjoying every one of those tickets and one will be a big winner one day. I know I'm only 23 so I'm probably more of an attraction to women than they are, but you only live once, as they say! These hopeless guys should just get off their asses and stop moaning and get on with life, but I suppose for most of them they are really past it. The world belongs to the young, don't you agree Hillary, or are you past it too?

- Lawrence the Lottery player.

Dear Lawrence,

Aren't you just the cat's whiskers, my Petal. Hillary is glad to see that you are only 23 as it helps explain your arrogance. We were all 23 once, and next year it will just be a memory for you too. Normal men have emotions, just as normal women do. That is why men write in with their emotional problems. It's a bit of a release for them. That is what these sorts of columns are about, my precious Lawrence. However, you do show me that you also are a loving person,

Lawrence, unfortunately it is only for yourself. Have you ever thought about changing your name to Narcissus? Hillary will bet you can't walk past a mirror without checking your reflection either. Ever heard the expression 'You've got tickets on yourself'? Well you certainly have, and it's not all lottery tickets. Your time is coming Lawrence the lottery lover. Now please go outside and play.

*

Dear Hillary,
The story I am writing you is true and I think everyone needs to know there is good and bad everywhere in the world. Not just bad here. I get sick of all the moans and groans that come from all your writers and how they have been ripped off or left in the lurch by some Thai girl. Perhaps they should be more careful. I think a lot of the people who get ripped off ask for it.
- Financial Freddie.

Dear Financial Freddie,
As you correctly point out, there is good and bad everywhere and Thailand is no different from anywhere else as far as that is concerned. The difference here seems to be that the foreigners come here and forget all good business sense, and are all blinded by the bevy of beauty that

surrounds them? Checking one's brain in at the immigration counter in Bangkok seems to be a very real situation. I often wonder if they remember to pick it up again when they leave.

*

Now please do not rush to the conclusion that I am being judgmental in Thailand's bedroom stakes. I do think these girls do a fantastic job in bringing people to Thailand to spend their money here. Sales of houses, gold chains, motorcycles and cars would dip alarmingly if the likely lads stopped coming over. But as Ms Hillary says, 'You don't go to a hardware shop if you want to buy cheese!'

By the way, if you want to read the best book on the Good Time Girls get a copy of Stephen Leather's *Private Dancer* or look out for *Miss Bangkok* by Bua Boonmee and Nicola Pierce. They should be made compulsory reading for all new arrivals!

~

Mistaken Identity

A RECENT ITEM IN THE *Pattaya Mail* newspaper concerned a male tourist who saw a young Thai woman walking in an area well known for its nightlife. The tourist was obviously bursting with pent-up hormones and was reported in the newspaper article as being drunk. A gigantic cultural misconception was about to happen.

The article said, 'Student intends to prosecute Irishman who drunkenly fondled her.' It continued: 'An Irishman who drunkenly fondled a university student was detained in custody when the 21-year-old girl said she intended pressing charges against him for assault. Police were called out just after midnight on 9 April when it was reported that a foreign tourist had obscenely groped a Thai woman at Soi Pattayaland, on Second Road.

'The victim, given the alias Miss Nid, was a third year student at the University of the Thai Chamber of Commerce. She was in tears, and identified the perpetrator, who was standing nearby, shirtless and in a state of drunkenness.

'Nid said that she had come to stay with her aunt in Pattaya during the school vacation, and had a holiday job selling leather at a shop near the scene. She was waiting for a baht bus with a friend to go back home. The accused and a friend were walking towards them with beer bottles in their hands, and appeared to be drunk. As he was passing, he hugged her and fondled her genitals and buttocks. She screamed for help. He responded by shouting that she was no different from a bargirl and that he could get sexual favours at any time.

'He admitted to the police that he had groped Nid, saying that he was drunk. He had been drinking, and when he saw Nid he thought she was a bargirl and that it would be normal to hug her and fondle her and ask her for sex.

'Nid has insisted on taking legal action, and the police have detained the man.'

So here we have an inebriated young buck, in an area of Pattaya where 'service girls' are everywhere, and mistakes another young Thai woman for one who would welcome his sexual attention. Big mistake.

This is not a one-off incident. The problem occurs because the tourists (and some ex-pat residents, I have to admit) presume that because there are so many good-time girls who are not averse to a roll in the hay (after certain financial details have been agreed upon), then all Thai girls are also similarly available. Nothing could be much further from the truth.

No matter what you may have read about the 'acceptability' of working as a service girl, the vast majority hide their employment from their parents, as such a form of work is simply not socially acceptable, especially in the Northeast (Isan), where most of the service girls have their home villages. My own wife, not a service girl, but who comes from Isan, was taunted by one of the local lads in her village on one trip home that since she lived in Pattaya, she was just another Pattaya prostitute. She was so incensed that she reported this to the local police, who indicted the lad and enforced a fine, which his family had to pay. If prostitution was so socially acceptable, the initial taunt would not have happened, nor the police response to the complaint. Think about it.

Now that is what happens in the impoverished Northeast. What do you think is the situation with the more affluent families in Bangkok? Work as a service girl is even less socially acceptable, hence the umbrage and outrage shown by the young woman in the newspaper item.

In some ways, you have to feel sorry for the young tourist. Thai women are very alluring, service girls or otherwise, and both groups tend to dress in an overtly sexually attractive way. Looking 'sexy' is acceptable, but not raunchy! There is a difference.

'Good girls' wear pantyhose to work, and beneath the plunging décolletage there will be a clinging top, which is often skin coloured, to add to the visual effect. I should also add that Thai women seem to go into a bra at about eight years of age, despite lack of any discernable chest development, and a bra is even more important than the 'never leave home without it' American Express card.

Any woman you see without a bra is either a service girl, or a 'katoey' (transvestite) just to confuse the issue even further.

There is yet another cultural factor which has led to the belief that bar work is acceptable, and that is the fact that Thais will go out of their way not to comment on others. In fact practising Buddhists are exhorted not to think or speak badly about people. 'You should not say anything, even if they are bad. It's not our problem,' my wife added, when I discussed this concept with her.

In other words, the bad karma sits with the individual for following such a chosen 'profession', but commenting on it would make bad karma for the finger pointer. In addition, in Thailand, people are accepted for what they are 'now', rather than remaining pariah forever as happens in some areas of the Western world.

It is back to the 'the more you know, the less you understand' situation, as is always the case with *farang*s attempting to comprehend the convoluted Thai culture. Nothing is really what it seems on the outside, and as a foreigner living here, you have to be prepared to drop your own preconceived ideas. Unless you have grown up in the village, speak Thai as your first language, and understand the Thai family culture, you will never, ever, really know. As my wife says, 'Farang, they think too much.'

So now you can probably see that prostitution is not acceptable (and incidentally against the law), but it is not acceptable to comment adversely on anyone who is a prostitute. This is why it appears to the Western eye that being a prostitute in Thailand is acceptable! An Eastern version of Joseph Heller's Catch-22.

However, back to the lad being sued by the Thai lady. Also in typical Thai fashion, a monetary value will be placed on the embarrassment suffered by the young lady, and the tourist, if he knows what is good for him, will agree to an out-of-court settlement, plus a few baht in the envelope for the negotiating policeman. It will be cheaper than going to court, being found guilty, spending some time in jail, paying a hefty fine and legal fees and then being deported and having his passport stamped as persona non grata.

Incidentally, public drunkenness is not acceptable either!

~

Driving in Thailand

SINCE 'THAI' MEANS 'FREE', THAILAND is then the land of the free. This makes for a free and easy attitude and free and easy living, which unfortunately also carries over into the Thai traffic. Driving in Thailand then becomes a very different situation from that which we are all used to.

Whereas in the West we have red-light cameras to ensure compliance with coming to a stop at the red light, the Thai driver considers traffic lights to be only 'advisory' at best. Or to be totally ignored at worst. I can personally guarantee that when you slip through the light at the last possible second as it turns to red from amber, there will be at least three other vehicles following you through.

Of course, this means that the first vehicles away on the green from the intersecting street have to contend with the 'last across' group coming across their bows the other way. Since these are mainly motorcycles, you have ample opportunity for carnage. Or should that be motorbikenage?

The 'advisory' sign concept also covers the yellow or white lines in the middle of the road. Thais will pass on blind bends, before the brow of a hill, in fact anywhere. It makes no difference that there are double unbroken lines in the centre of the road and there is an 18-wheeler truck approaching. Lights are flashed and through they go. Many end up as members of the 'Do not pass Go' club and claim early on their life insurance.

A mention of headlamp flashers is in order here. In general, in the West, a flash of the headlamps at an intersection, for example, is taken as a polite 'after you'. This is definitely not the case in Thailand, where a flash of the headlamps indicates 'I am coming through, no matter what or who you are.'

And that brings me to another item. Every so often you will be driving along and begin to notice a policeman on every intersection or T-junction. Eventually you will be stopped at one and will wait there for sometimes 20 minutes to let the cavalcade of vehicles carrying royalty to go through unimpeded. I have been hoping to see the King at one of these times, but so far have not been lucky. That and the fact they come through at around 100 km/h and all the cars have dark windows.

Now there are some phrases in the ex-pat community that go, 'You know you've been in Thailand too long when ...' One of those is 'When you look both ways before you cross a one-way street!' Nothing could be closer to the truth.

If a motorcycle wants to go up a one-way street the wrong way, they just do it. So here you are coming out of a service station and joining a one-way carriageway. You have to turn left to join the traffic flow and are gazing intently out of the driver's window to slot into a gap in the oncoming traffic. As you pull out from the driveway—bang! You have just collected a motorcycle coming the wrong way up the road in the nearside (kerb) lane.

If you are lucky, the rider(s) won't be injured and have insurance. If you are not lucky, the (principal) rider will be 12 years old, without license or insurance, and will have broken his leg. Since you have the larger vehicle, and you are a *farang*, you will be expected to take care of the 12-year-old and get him to the nearest (private) hospital, where you will be held responsible for the bill(s). This is why you need insurance to cover this eventuality.

By the way, if the injuries are such that it will take more than 21 days for recovery, then this becomes a criminal case, you will be found guilty, and you will be deported. The only way around this problem is again a matter of private arrangement between the injured and yourself, represented by your insurance company. The company will offer so much on your behalf, which won't be accepted until you put a little sweetener on top, and something in an envelope for the friendly policeman, who actually has been helping you escape deportment! Look both ways before entering a one-way street!

Have I put you off driving in Thailand yet? If I haven't, then consider this—around 85% of vehicles on the roads are motorcycles. They are everywhere, sliding through between the cars, pickups and buses. To be able to do this, they have very short clip-on handlebars on each side, so that the width of the motorcycle is no greater than the rider's shoulders. If the person can get through, the motorcycle can too. This is done at around 50 km/h, so you must never swerve to let the motorcycle on your left get through, as there are two more squeezing through on your right. Again, do not hit a motorcycle.

So far I have been dealing with *farangs* driving their cars on Thailand's roads. There are however a group of resident ex-pats who ride motorcycles, and a large number of visitors who have hired big bikes for their holiday. It is not a case of 'if' you have an accident in Thailand, it is merely 'when' you are going to have that accident.

The statistics bandied about are that we send two motorcyclists home in wooden boxes each week. This I cannot verify, but I can tell you that we see many young lads at the hospital with multiple injuries after motorcycle accidents. Many of them die. You can see this group any evening in South Pattaya, full of beer and bravado, astride large capacity motorcycles, far larger than anything they have ridden in their home country, and blipping the throttle aggressively. Generally they don't wear a helmet, but I would probably go along with this, as there is precious little brain inside to protect.

Since this is a rental bike, the helmet is also of the quality of an ice cream bucket, and just as protective.

Motorcycles, because of their nimbleness, have also decided that they are not limited to only using the roadway—there is the footpath as well, especially in the 5pm commuter rush. There is no safety for the pedestrian on the sidewalk!

If there is a problem caused by two wheel devices on Thailand's roads, it just doesn't end there. Three wheel devices, and there are several, are also a problem.

Take first the motorcycle with sidecar attached. These are not the well-engineered items that ply the British roads, but strange metal cages hung on the side of the motorcycle. Most of the framework is made from reinforcing rod used in buildings—some obviously stolen from buildings! These sidecars are used to transport a wide variety of goods and people, and it is not uncommon to see one happily going down the road with a complete family in the sidecar, with the oldest member sitting regally on a plastic chair in the middle of it. Holding the family dog.

For some reason not known to me, in the act of attaching the sidecar to the frame of the motorcycle, all the electrical connections to the motorcycle are disconnected, so at night there are no tail lights. Just another hazard! These motorcycle outfits are also used to tow boats and water scooters, and you will come across a string of scooters on their trailers all being towed by one outfit. At 10 km/h, and with no lights on any part of it. Accidents between cars and water scooters are not unheard of.

Then there is the vehicle much-loved by tourists; the tuk-tuk. This three-wheeled vehicle has one front wheel, and two rears. Powered by a water-cooled Daihatsu twin cylinder engine of 400cc, this noisy and smoky device probably blows bigger holes in the ozone layer than all of Thailand's manufacturing industries combined. It also has brakes only on the rear wheels, and in the rain happily slides into the car in front with everything locked on. You pray that you are not the front car.

One front and two rears is also the format for a wonderful Thai device known as a Skylab. Where this name comes from, I do not know, and even the manufacturer was unable to tell me. This beast is like an enlarged tuk-tuk, with a 1,200cc engine (usually Toyota Corolla), running back to the car's gearbox and differential and rear axle. The handlebars look like something out of Easy Rider, 'ape hangers' at their best, complete with suitably endowed riders. These are most usually seen in the country provinces, but everything that was written about tuk-tuks applies to these as well, especially as they are larger and faster.

But it doesn't end there. There are other motorised devices that must be avoided. Again three-wheelers, but this time two in the front and one at the rear. These resemble a motorcycle (from which they are derived) mated to a two-wheeled cart at the front. The rider sits astride the motorcycle seat and steers using a horizontal bar attached to the cart, which has a motorcycle twist grip throttle incorporated in it at one end. These are often used by the garbage 'recyclers', and will stop at any time close to a rubbish bin, have no lights and the riders are oblivious of any other traffic.

Road users without lights are always a hazard in this country, and in this category you have to include wandering elephants. Large amorphous grey masses, without any visible tail light, that ply both major and minor roads. In confrontational meetings, the elephant generally wins, other than with railway trains. And that is yet another hazard for the *farang* driver.

Trains (*rot fai*) cross roads and vice versa at unmanned crossings, at which 90% do not have operating warning lights. Or such as the one close to my home, which has a weak, probably one candlepower light, which burns 24 hours a day, and is therefore ignored by all road users. Other than the ones that manage to collect a train. And that is about once a month.

That just about leaves pedestrians as the final hazards, and they certainly are that. The Thai pedestrians are not too bad. They just run across three or four lanes of traffic, and seem to make it unscathed, other than the final time! However, it is the *farang* pedestrians who pose the greatest hazard. Having come from countries like the UK, where the pedestrian can wave one foot over the zebra crossing and bring all traffic to a halt, these people have a very rude awakening.

The Thai motoring community, using Thai logic, has already worked out that since there are no zebras in

Thailand other than in zoos, there is therefore no need to stop. There are no zebras crossing. So the drivers do not stop at the pedestrian foot over the crossing, with the end result being shaking, screaming foreign tourists cowering on the pavement after a vehicular near-miss. They are then ready to be collected by a taxi motorcycle using the footpath to avoid the traffic on the roadway!

Apart from those minor problems, driving in Thailand is easy. Just never look sideways, or otherwise you have to acknowledge that there are other vehicles on the road, and you might be forced to give way. Only 'might' however!

~

Visa Problems

ALMOST EVERY EX-PAT IN THAILAND will, after a period of time, find themselves with a Thai friend, be that male or female, or in between. It doesn't matter. What does matter is that for that same Thai friend to visit your home country, you are going to need a visa for him/her.

I have experience in applying for a visa for both Australia and the UK, and like many things in Thailand, this can be difficult, but this time it is not Thai bureaucracy that is to blame—but our own ex-pat ones.

Let me explain the Australian side first. I had been invited to go to a conference in Cairns, on Australia's Barrier Reef, and I thought it would be a good time to take my (then) fiancé (later my wife) to show her a bit of Australia, the country where I had lived for 40 years while learning to speak through my nose.

I had no intention of returning there to stay. In fact, since I hold a UK passport, I had to get a re-entry permit myself, to get back into Australia again. This was going to be no problem, I was sure. I could prove I had been a resident in Australia, and I had perfected speaking through my nose so well, everybody naturally assumed I was an Australian.

However, my girlfriend would need a visitor's visa to cover a one week's stay. I rang the visa section of the Australian Embassy and was put through to an Australian-sounding lady, so that I could explain what I needed. Hearing the Aussie voice was reassuring. At least the person on the other end of the phone would be able to understand me.

I went straight to the point, asking what we needed to get a visitor's visa for my fiancé? Back came the rejoinder, 'Can you prove the relationship?'

'Eh? What do you mean prove?' My medical mind was wondering whether this was going to lead up to having to prove an exchange of body fluids or what?

'Joint bank account, joint electricity account, joint telephone bills, or similar,' said the Aussie voice at the other end.

'Well no. We have separate bank accounts and the telephone and electricity bills go to the owner of the house I rent.'

At that, the voice launched into a tirade about how these young Thai girls get older males like me to take them to Australia where they run away and join the sex industry! At that, I began to get angry, and politely told the voice not to bother, as neither of us would be going. I did point out that as I was a doctor employed by the largest private hospital on the Eastern Seaboard, I was not in the habit of taking young Thai girls to Australia so they could join the sex industry.

I did not tell my girlfriend exactly why I had dropped the idea of the trip to Australia, as I knew she would be even more livid than I was at such blatant racial prejudice.

Having decided to forget about Australia (and I have not been back since, by the way) we decided it would be better to go to the UK so she could meet her future mother-in-law, who lives in the north of Scotland. This would require a visitor's visa for the UK, and from all reports, this could be an even greater problem than the Australian Kangaroo court had been.

However, we were getting smarter, and by asking around in the ex-pat community, we were reliably informed that the worry was the girl not returning, and we would have to show that she had reason to return. The usual reasons being her children, or real estate holdings. There was also 'the interview' we were told, where she is taken into one room and grilled, while you are in another. If the answers do not match up at the end, the visa will be denied.

I could see that this was looking as if it was going to be a problem. My fiancé had neither children in the village, nor real estate portfolio. So we began to collect as many documents as we could to show that we were a couple (photographs in the local paper helped there), plus affidavits from prominent UK persons in Thailand, such as the office bearers in the British Chamber of Commerce, Thailand would look impressive.

We got letters from her place of employment and details of how she was on a traineeship programme. My sister, living in the UK, signed guarantees that she would repatriate my fiancé if something went wrong while we were over there. Eventually we had several sheets of paper with important looking letterheads. But what about the interview?

We sat down and discussed this. Sure, we could pretend there was a sick mother she was looking after or similar ruses, but neither my fiancé nor I wanted to risk telling porky pies, which any trained interviewer would be able to break. We decided that if we just told the truth, then our answers would coincide.

We went to Bangkok to make our application, getting there around 8.30am, handed in our weighty file and then found that we had just scored visa applicants ticket number 61. There were only another 60 couples ahead of us. We sat down and the long wait began. We looked at some of the other couples and began to get a feeling of pity for visa officers. The skinhead with tattoos all over the back of his cranium with his Thai girlfriend in the shortest mini and fluorescent green boob tube would surely attract additional scrutiny. They must have been an item for at least several days.

Eventually at 11.30am, with our backsides suitably numb, we were called to the window, and together we were asked a few questions by the British male and Thai female visa officers. They looked at our paperwork and my UK passport and said everything was in order, and we could go.

'Don't we have to be interviewed?' I asked.

'No sir, we will post the Thai passport back to you with the visitor's visa.'

It was difficult not to burst out laughing; we had been keeping ourselves in such a mental state of anxiety, and suddenly it was all over! A few weeks later when we went on that first trip, we arrived at Heathrow and joined the long queue for 'Aliens'. I said I would stay with her, just in case she had any communication problems, and then when she was through I would go to the 'Returning Residents' very much shorter queue.

We watched as the different immigration officers dealt with the hopefuls entering the UK. It was obvious that some visitors were certainly getting the full treatment. Some were even being escorted away, being led to their departing plane, one imagined. And then it was our turn. I explained that I had a British passport, but was there to help with communication if it were needed. He looked at the visa, asked my fiancé why she was coming to the UK and where she would be staying, and that was it.

'I hope you have a pleasant stay in the UK,' were his parting words.

I thanked him and made to join my rightful queue, but he stopped me, taking my passport and saying, 'No need for that, Sir. You can come through here. Welcome home.'

We still talk about that first visa (we have had more since then) and our entry into the UK. But I am still angry at the treatment we received from the Aussies. There is no need to treat anyone disrespectfully over the phone. Poor risk applicants are soon weeded out when the applications hit the desk in Bangkok. People ringing with requests for advice should not be treated as if they were human traffickers.

~

Dtat Pom

HAVING MY HAIR CUT HAS been the bane of my life. As a young boy, I had thick black hair that had a pronounced 'cow's lick' at the front, making it stand up (almost like the fashionable '*khunying*' style adopted by high society ladies of a certain age in Thailand).

My earliest memories are of sitting on the wooden board that the barber placed over the arms of the big chair, while my father stood there saying, 'Can you do something with this child's hair?'

Consequently, in my formative years I grew up thinking there was something wrong, or even strange, with my hair. It resulted in my being unable to talk to my barber on a normal client-to-provider basis, and my fortnightly mumbling became, 'Can you do something with my hair?' as my less than specific instructions. Really it is remarkable just how one's parental tapes extend into one's adult life.

Having grown much older since those days, the once luxuriant black locks have turned a vague shade of grey (or if I were totally truthful, a decided shade of white). The locks are also far from luxuriant, and indeed are missing from certain parts of my cranium.

This has produced a few results.

Firstly, the 'cow's lick' has gone. Secondly, the 'thinning scissors' are no longer required. And thirdly, I only have to visit the barber once every four weeks. However, the basic communication difficulty remains. If I could not be specific to native English speaking barbers, what hope would I have with native Thai speakers?

At one stage, I even showed photographs of people with what I thought were good haircuts to my wife, suggesting that perhaps I should show these to the barber. She laughed a lot, saying unkind things like, 'But he's got far more hair than you've got.'

The story of Samson and Delilah came flooding back, with all the emasculating phobias that trips to the barber can produce. I waited six weeks before my next visit, but I had to succumb, as it was either a haircut or a violin, and violins are expensive.

Fortunately, I spotted that there was a barber's at the top end of my little *soi* in Jomtien. I made several surreptitious reconnoitres and it looked clean enough. There was also a sign in the window with a large 50 and some 'wriggle-writing' on it. Checking with my wife confirmed that this was indeed 50 baht for a haircut.

At this stage, I should point out that I have a strong Scottish heritage, and the thought of paying 200 baht (or more) for the number of hairs I have left now, is over the top, in more ways than one. 50 baht looked like the bargain I was looking for.

So one Sunday morning, having memorised the phrase *'Dat phom'* (hair cut), I approached the local barbershop. Opening the door I found a row of chairs along one wall and two barber's chairs along the other. All chairs were full to overflowing. A quick spurt of mental arithmetic left me in no doubt that this represented a wait of around two hours. Obviously, I was not the first to spot that at 50 baht, this was a real bargain! I decided that I could wait for another week.

The following Sunday, but much earlier in the day, I entered Khun Bargain Barbers again. There were only four waiting, and two barbers furiously electro-shearing young Thai boys to give them the traditional shaved skull look, but without the topknot. I began to panic, fearing that they might give me the same style. Perhaps this explained the 50 baht!

Finally it was my turn. *'Dtat pom'* I said nervously, to which the barber replied, in perfect Thai, several phrases, none of which I recognised. It was back to, 'Can you do something with (what's left of) my hair?' But this time in mime.

Writing that last sentence reminds me just how much living in Thailand brings out the art of mime in the non-Thai speaker. I've become an expert, finding toilets with just the wiggle of one index finger held by the thumb and index of the other hand. Universally understandable! Forget 'Hong naam yu tii nai?' The wiggling finger can do it all.

So Khun 50 Baht Barber set about my head with shears, scissors and comb, and then swiped my sideburns and neck with his open razor. Silently I prayed that he did not have some deep-seated dislike of *farangs*. You know the sort of thing—family (dis)honour after his sister ran off with a Frenchman or something. I found myself gripping the arms of the chair in a vice-like grip, unable to move my head, in case it fell off my shoulders, but such worries were not needed. Neck stubble and even the hairy bits on my ears were attended to, and a little hedge pruning inside my nostrils, as a follow-up.

But the 50 baht special did not end there. The next I knew was that my arms were being rapidly flexed, fingers pulled, neck prodded and shoulders slapped, and then that ritual of thumping you with the hands together, producing the sound that heralds the end of the session.

Khun Bargain Barber stood back smiling. I arose, also smiling, and paid him the 50 baht and returned home to show my wife the results of my linguistic skills in the barbershop.

'Why didn't you get him to make it shorter on top?' said she. I just asked him if he could do something with my hair, I replied lamely, before I was again set upon with the family scissors, but I have to admit the end result was fine.

Since those days, the price has gone up to 60 baht, and every time it is still too long on top and my wife corrects it. When one day I learn how to ask for it shorter, she may even find herself redundant!

~

Modesty

THE FIRST TIME I VISITED a beach in Thailand was many years ago in Pattaya. I must have arrived on the sand very shortly after a ferry had gone down, as there were about 100 Thais all swimming towards the shore. They had obviously been caught unawares, as all were fully dressed, just as they would have been on any ferry headed to the islands off Pattaya.

I looked at this sight, wondering if I should immediately plunge into the waves, or give myself enough time to at least slip out of my shirt and trousers. It was then that I noticed that nobody on the beach was paying any notice at all to the ferry passengers. No screaming, no attempts at rescue. Nothing.

I stood there amazed, as the odd pair of swimmers started coming ashore, most dressed in sopping black T-shirts and jeans, to then walk up to a deck chair with their friends and plop themselves down. Much laughter, another bottle of beer and *som tam* was brought and so the show went on.

Inadvertently, I had stumbled across one of the prime rules of Thai dress codes: 'When you go to the beach for a swim, you go in fully dressed.'

Over the years I have now seen this phenomenon many times. However, it is not all just modesty, though any Thai girl who goes swimming in a bikini is thought of as immodest. It goes much deeper than that. The simple answer is that the Thais do not want to go brown!

Apparently, the gorgeous brown skin aspired to by all *farang*s is not liked by the Thais. The deeper the hue, the more it shows that you are from the agricultural working class which toils in the sun, planting rice. Hence the total cover-up on the beach.

By the way, if you need some proof of this colour bias, watch any Thai TV programme and you will find the principal sponsor will be a cosmetic company selling 'whitening' creams, lotions and other pastes and potions. Thai photographic models are always whiter than white—and it is all through bleach for the beach.

Now when you mention Thai modesty and Thai girls, there is a tendency for the novice *farang* to get confused. Are these the same girls who will dance naked in any go-go bar? It would seem on the surface that modesty does not exist in the Thai language, but it does. In fact, last year there was a great to-do over a fashion parade in Bangkok, where one model's nipple did a brief peek-a-boo as she sashayed down the catwalk. This made front-page news—but any photograph to prove the censorial point obviously did not. The incident was called being 'un-Thai'.

Another example this year was one starlet who attended a provincial film festival in a very revealing dress. Howls of outrage were heard all over the country. Not only were there several millimetres of skin showing (no nipples I hasten to add), but it looked as if she had no underwear on either! (She was later nicknamed 'seaweed') Gasp! The immediate result was that the director of the film cut any footage of the aspiring actress out of the movie.

It did not end there. The actress was a university student and she was then publicly reprimanded by the university authorities. As an attempt to mollify the frenzied mob, the offending dress was brought out again to show it had knickers that were built-in. It only looked as if the wearer was nude underneath. But it was too late. The Letters to the Editor were ablaze with outrage, though a few moderates did suggest that the event had been blown out of proportion.

So how do you equate having apparently acceptably nude go-go dancers on one hand and public paranoia over a flash of nipple? Or even presumed lack of underwear? This makes the Janet Jackson and Justin Timberlake 'wardrobe malfunction' tame by comparison.

The answer is quite simple. Nude go-go dancers do not exist. There is legislation to outlaw such vicarious practices, and there are organised police raids on establishments breaking the law. These are so well organised and rehearsed that the establishment is usually given as much pre-raid information as the local boys in brown. Consequently, by the time of the raid, the dancers are all covered up, and everybody is happy. Justice has been seen to be done, one of the cornerstones of democracy, you will all agree.

However, I do believe that Thai girls are inherently modest, no matter how they might seem to the wide-eyed outsider. Those who have enjoyed an evening of horizontal folk dancing are staggered to find that in the morning, the young lady will appear from the shower, completely wrapped in a towel. The brassiere is then put on over the towel, and the towel gently tugged out from under the bra, to ensure there is no repeat of the aforesaid 'wardrobe accidents'! The evening's entertainment was 'business' but the post-event performance reverts to traditional Thai modesty.

Even my little three year old is told by her mother that she 'must always be polite' and she is sent to bring a pair of knickers before she goes outside. And I agree. This dress code will be firmly adhered to. Feather boas, as used in the West will not be accepted. Modesty must prevail. Father, mother and the Thai legislation will insist on it.

~

Miss One Minute

I HAVE BEEN A MOTOR racer for many years. Too many years, when I think back, having had my first race in 1965, and 'officially' retiring in 1997. But I immediately donned the race suit this year (2007) when I was offered a drive in the Four Hour Race at the Bira Circuit!

By the time I was ready to leave Australia at the end of 1997, I had also been the Medical Assessor for many years for the Confederation of Australian Motor Sport, itself affiliated with the FIA, the world legislators of motor sport.

Looking at the international calendar that year, I noted that there was a race at the Bira circuit coinciding with my holidays and a request for an introduction to the Asian motor racing scene was done by the Confederation of Australian Motor Sport on my behalf. This resulted in an invitation to attend from the organisers, Grand Prix International, including being met at the airport. Being of common birth I naturally accepted such a 'royal' reception.

I was indeed met by a Khun Chavalit, who became a great friend, but who unfortunately passed away from cancer this year. Sorely missed. But back in 1997, Chavalit picked me up and took me straight to the Bira Circuit. There came the first cultural shock.

If you are a guest Down Under, this results in greetings which are a perfunctory, 'G'Day mate' and a handshake. However, Thailand, as you are aware, is quite different, and I was not quite ready for it then. There appeared to be a never-ending conga line of smiling, bowing and *wai*-ing and people wanting to exchange business cards with this person from Australia. I had so many that at one stage I think I was probably recycling someone else's!

Surreptitious glances at my overflowing fist showed I had met the owner, the Clerk of the Course and his assistant, the doctor and nurse, the Chief Marshal and a whole squadron of people whose name cards were all in Thai. I had however, at that stage, found out how to order a beer and find the toilet; the bare essentials.

Returning from the loo I was given a bright yellow spray jacket by the Chief Marshal, emblazoned with the name Singha Beer, and it was insisted that I wear it. No sooner had I got it on, than I was forcibly propelled on to the grid where there was a huge line-up of drivers, officials and beautiful brolly dollies. I tried to infiltrate the back line, but to no avail. I was positioned centre front. TV cameras zoomed in and an announcer began talking in Thai. It was then that the truth sank in—I was supposed to open the meeting!

As photographers popped their flashguns, I stood there with not a clue as regards what I was expected to do, but I smiled. Smile? My dental records have been translated into several Asian languages. Someone gave me a piece of string attached to several helium filled balloons and a banner and gave me a swift elbow in the ribs at the appropriate moment. As the banner floated skywards the cameras turned away and my 'official' duties were over, I presumed, so I removed the jacket.

No sooner had the first race finished when the Chief Marshal was again at my side, brandishing the yellow jacket once more. 'Put on' he said tersely and I was dragged on to the podium with the winners of the first event. Again it was TV and flashguns and I applauded loudly and stood back. The swift elbow came out again with an even terser *sotto voce*: 'Present trophies!'

Wearing my best smile again, I began presenting trophies and garlands. With some luck, the right drivers may have received the correct trophies, but I smiled for TV, oh boy did I smile!

Another difference between Thai style motor racing and that of the Land of Oz lies in the warning to the drivers that the race will soon be underway. Instead of dog-eared boards stating 2 Minutes, 1 Minute and 30 Seconds, Thailand has a bevy of leggy ladies who parade in front of the field at the appropriate time. I also noticed that Miss 30 seconds was faster than the other two, who did not have to contend with revving engines and drivers with the 'red mist' over the eyes!

I watched the start from the observation tower and I noticed some male appreciation of these babes with the boards, with what appeared to be impromptu voting amongst the officials. I ventured that in my opinion Miss One Minute looked the best. This brought forth the vigorous rejoinder, 'You'd want more than one minute with her!'

At the end of the meeting I was shown the telecast of the meeting, going out to every lounge room and bar in Thailand. The opening ceremony was being played, and there, front and centre, was this figure in the yellow jacket. It was Andy Warhol who said that everyone would be famous for 15 minutes in their lifetime. I have had my quarter of an hour. There on Thai national TV was this Australian doctor, with the script along the bottom of the screen: 'Dr Iain Corness—FIA.'

Now, what the ultimate governing body of world motor sport would have said about the medical officer from the Antipodes leap-frogging his way into the top echelon of the sport, I do not know, but I was rather chuffed!

When it was time to return to Bangkok, I thanked my very gracious hosts, who had not only made me welcome, but a 'star' at the same time. But there was more in store yet! As I was waved off by the Assistant Clerk of Course, a folded piece of paper was pressed into my palm, which I put in my pocket. Later on the trip back, I opened it to find the name and phone number of Miss One Minute. Only Thailand could offer such hospitality, and with a capital 'H'. And did I ring Miss One Minute? Ah, that is another story for another day!

~

If you think you get a good welcome in
Bangkok, try Esarn, or Isan, in the Northeastern
region, populated by the most incredibly friendly
people.

Esarn

THERE IS AN UNFORTUNATE TENDENCY for us *farangs* to inhabit the major centres in Thailand; Bangkok, Pattaya, Chiang Mai and Phuket. This is all fairly understandable, as these are the regions in which there is work for the ex-pats, and the local population is better versed in English.

However, there is much more to Thailand than just the major centres. There is one very densely populated area called Esarn, or Isan, or even Isaan. Remember there is no exact transliteration from Thai to English. 44 letters do not fit into 26!

The following is a true account of my first visit to Esarn, that impoverished Northeast of Thailand, from which 90% of the ladies who frequent the bars in the aforesaid Bangkok, Pattaya, Chiang Mai and Phuket appear to have come from.

A few years ago, having rather overdone things, I was told by my doctor (yes, even doctors have doctors) to take a holiday. Now, from the outset it should be noted that I have no hidden masochistic streaks. I have always said that for me, 'roughing it' was a camp stretcher in the foyer of a five star hotel, so when I said I would like to go and see a little of the Esarn region of Thailand for this enforced vacation, I had no thoughts of backpacking or sleeping in rough huts on a dusty terrain. I leave doing things the 'difficult way' to those who carry Lonely Planet guides as their personal bibles. I am more likely to be carrying a guide to selecting fine wines! Not that I was expecting any in Esarn.

What had prompted me to think about experiencing Esarn was a book that had been recommended to me—*The Force of Karma* by Pira Sudham, a well known proponent of the poor people of the country's Northeastern region.

The city of Khon Kaen is billed as the 'capital' of the Esarn region, so I decided to go there. There was no planning. It was real 'spur of the moment' stuff. Keep reading and experience a different and delightful area of the Kingdom, I told myself.

Khon Kaen is 450 kilometres from Bangkok, so that is around 600 kilometres from Pattaya, and you can fly there from Bangkok via Thai International, which has four daily flights there (and return), or travel by road. I chose the road mode, where you can have the choice of the 'scenic' and shorter route (but longer travelling time) via single carriageway roads like highway 331 at the Eastern Seaboard, through to 304 to Khorat (Nakhon Ratchasima) and then up to Khon Kaen, or the easier divided road motorways, via numbers 7, to 9 to 1 to 2 and straight into Khon Kaen.

I took the hassle-free motorway and made Khon Kaen in five and a half hours on the road travelling time. The next part of my exploration trip was probably one of the most amazing aspects of Esarn. There in Khon Kaen is one of the flashest, ritziest, glitziest five star hotels in the Kingdom—the Sofitel Raja Orchid Khon Kaen, to give it its full title.

This is an almost 300-room hotel boasting 32 executive suites and even what is described as a five bedroom bi-level penthouse. Not being 'bi' I passed that one over. There were ten restaurants plus a disco, a sophisticated cocktail lounge, a karaoke studio and an underground bar with micro-brewery run by a German brewmaster (or should that be 'brewmeister').

Of course it also has huge conference and banquet areas, and a business centre—I didn't use any of them either—this was my holiday. I parked my bag in one of the executive suites, room 802, and I can recommend it! As I said, I don't believe in roughing it.

Having arrived at 6pm, after a shower and freshen up, I had some snacks in the 'Underground' eatery and washed it down with a couple of their beers. There's a light lager style, a dark beer and a wheat beer. The dark was a nice drop, and at 4.5% alcohol you can even have a couple of steins. Then I had a look at the entertainment facilities—all certainly top class, but being in Khon Kaen for the first time I thought I should have a look at what was outside the hotel.

Tip number 1: at night, don't bother. Apart from the Charoen Hotel's cocktail lounge stocked with singers in skimpy costumes, the best of everything nightlife-wise is in the Sofitel. Believe me.

The next morning it was a trip to the Tourism Authority of Thailand, Northeastern office, where a very helpful young lady told me all about the tourist attractions in the Khon Kaen area and gave me enough brochures (in English) to write several articles if I so wished. I didn't, but I can tell you where to find the famous dinosaur Siamotyrannus Isanensis (he's big), the Phra That Kham Kaen 19-metre-high *chedi* at Wat Jediyaphum, the Ubolrat Dam or the Koo Puai Noi Khmer complex. If you are into these, the TAT will point you in the right direction and give you a push!

But for me, it was time to discover the 'real' Khon Kaen, and what a wonderful eye-opener that turned out to be. In the mornings there is a local market area running between the Namuang and Klanguang roads. Do go! It is worth the heat just to receive the incredibly friendly welcome of the people there. There was not one footpath trader who did not want his or her photograph taken—and all with huge smiles, with or without teeth. It made no difference that I did not want to buy any of their 'stuffed on the spot' sausages, or 'killed as you watch' fish. They were just delighted that this *farang* was there, interacting with them and appreciating them for what they are—incredibly friendly people.

If you think you get a good welcome elsewhere in Thailand, try Esarn. There is nothing like it. Even the toothless old crones would want to pose, giving me great gaping grins—truly amazing, and yet I felt honoured to be amongst them.

In the afternoon, after a lunch and a lie down (I was supposed to be on holidays, remember) I decided to venture further afield and visited the Khon Kaen University, which is enormous. Not executed in the classic European sort of 'Grand Hall' architectural style, but numerous different colleges dotted all over the huge (5,000 *rai*— that's about 8 square kilometres) campus area. If of the academic bent, it would be a very interesting afternoon just being shown around the faculty facilities.

Wishing to recapture some of the spirit of the morning market, I then drove out of Khon Kaen to see what lay outside the civic environs. Good roads take you everywhere in a rural setting. In the industrialised areas such as Pattaya and Bangkok, it is easy to forget that Thailand is still mainly an agrarian economy, even if telecommunication towers are now appearing in the rice paddies. Along the roadsides indigenous people herd their cattle or drive along in the incredible local trucks, powered by a single cylinder stationary pump engine in the front, sputtering down the road with its one lung going *doonk-doonk-doonk*. Forget the tuk-tuks, these are *doonk-doonks*! Though I believe they are known as '*ee-tuns*' by the Esarn people.

I would pull up and wave my camera, to be greeted in return with those warm friendly smiles, not bashful, but open and amicable. I began to feel a warm love and appreciation for these rural dwellers. There was an honesty in their living that is not always present when 'modernism' takes over. Or 'globalisation', today's buzz word.

Travelling further afield and branching off the highway and down dusty dirt trails was where I found the non-urban Esarn people. Little villages with around 20-30 houses, complete with communal areas in front of the primitive wooden houses, populated with women, children and chickens, in no particular order lie scattered around. But they all had that wide open welcoming smile, even if the happy chooks did run away when the flash went off.

The wives and children of the local rice farmers made me welcome, without showing any real curiosity as to why this *farang* was there, obviously an oddity off the beaten track. I presented no threat to them, nor them to me. Small boys would run up and pose, while the man and wife passing by on the motorcycle waved. Was this how life used to be? Was this how life should be? I really do not have the answer—but it was certainly a beautiful feeling to step back in time and experience this genuine and honest reception.

To say that I was enchanted by the people of Esarn would be to put it mildly. They left me with a feeling that they had, without the use of micro-computers and fast food outlets, discovered the true meaning of life, while I was rushing around with fully charged gigabytes at 160 km/h, too fast to see where the 'real' world really was.

In retrospect, I may never step off my life's merry-go-round, but I do know people who have fallen off it, endlessly looking for the truth in life. I do also know people who have never got on that merry-go-round in the first place. Many of them live in Esarn. You would do yourself a favour to go and visit them. As Miss Terry Diner says in her Pattaya restaurant guide, 'Highly Recommended!'

~

Likay

THAI TV SOAP OPERAS, *likay*, are absolutely dreadful, if you cannot understand Thai. But if you can, they are even worse! That statement is one I read (and subsequently stole) and I have to agree with it. Totally. Fortunately, I belong to the first, non-understanding group, so I can actually sit with my wife for several minutes of each week's must-watch drama.

However, the other week we had an even better drama, right at the gate to our village. A *likay* performance!

It began with the erection of a stage in a vacant area, all professionally done with scaffolding, wooden boards and a tent-like structure over the top. Painted backdrops of luxurious castle interiors were next, with several stage lights, and then the *pièce de résistance*—the several metre high boom boxes at each side of the stage. The stage really was set for the evening's performance.

We arrived a trifle late, having had a prior dinner arrangement, but the entire village was there, and it was heaving. Everyone was sitting in rows facing the stage, and that was everyone from toothless crones to babes in nappies. Despite our tardiness, we were made welcome, and space found for us, and it was obvious from the mutters that the arrival of the *farang* was to make this event even more special.

The performers were wearing the most outrageous costumes you would ever see, all covered in sequins and bright glittery attachments. The trousers had exaggerated hips, standing out from the body, and make-up was de rigueur for both the female and male performers. The outfits made London's famous 'Pearly king and queen' look positively dowdy.

The principal performers all had microphones and were screaming Thai music in a strange sing-song wail, and a small percussion group with xylophone and cymbals provided the beat—all coming over at 120 decibels of distorted sound from the stereo boom boxes. This was an event you did not just listen to, or look at—this was an event you became an integral part of!

Being sung in Northeastern Thai, I had even less chance of understanding anything being intoned, but it wasn't really necessary. The plot was the same as in all Thai TV soaps. Bad girl takes good boy away from good girl. Fate intervenes and good girl meets good boy again. Good boy eventually realises that bad girl has tricked him. Bad girl is thrown out. Good girl is installed. Three cheers! Or in Thailand, that is three '*Chai yo*'s!'

But I did say that you, the audience, become an integral part of the show. Bad girl gets booed. Some will even leap on the stage and chastise her! Good girl is cheered, and she acknowledges this with demure *wais* from the stage. The actors are encouraged to greater heights with financial contributions from the crowd, who go up to the footlights to pass 20 baht notes to the appreciative performer. And where do the 20 baht notes go? With the performer singing away into his or her hand-held microphone, the money is taken by the free hand and slipped straight into the strange exaggerated hip sections of the trousers. They are special bulging pockets! Thai practicality again!

As the performance grinds on to the *dénouement* and dethroning of the bad girl, the audience is by now in a frenzy. Cat-calls, boos, jeers, and shaking fists are the order of the evening, and then cheers as she gets physically thrown off the stage into the audience. Some even begin lecturing her on her behaviour! It is an amazing sight.

I can imagine that 'theatre in the round' in the days of William Shakespeare must have been similar, with an interaction between performers and the audience, but that was 400 years ago. This is 2007.

It is claimed that *likay* performances are losing their popularity as Thailand becomes more globalised. *Spider Man* grossed more in its first week than any other movie in Thailand, surpassing even their own dramas such as *Tom Yum Goong*. However, this was not always the case. In one spectacular performance, a Thai man was arrested for burning down his house in anger because his wife attended a *likay* concert without him. Or perhaps she attended the *likay* with someone else? One never knows.

One website says there is a downturn in audience numbers because the main audience is made up of old people. Not so in my village. There were some oldies, and even the old *farang*, but the children were there in droves as well. I mean, where else can you see some lady being kicked off a stage and landing in the lap of some lucky member of the audience? Where else can you hound her back onto the stage, and be clapped by the crowd? Where else, other than in Thailand, and even in my Jomtien village?

~

Living in Fear of ED

It seems that a large percentage of ex-pat males in this country live in fear of ED; Erectile Dysfunction! Otherwise known as failing one's homework and often associated with Brewer's Droop. With so many young, gorgeous women around, this affliction must be life-threatening. Or life-altering at least.

Judging by the number of signs outside small medical clinics, Erectile Dysfunction, or ED, must be very prevalent in Thailand. The sign usually indicates the treatment as well, where you can take your choice from Viagra, Cialis or Levitra. It's all there on the sign. Salvation is through this clinic's doors. Hallelujah, ED has been conquered, just like we did with smallpox all those years ago.

I used to have a very old cat. Didn't do much, just slept under the back stairs most of the day. Got up a couple of times for a pee and something to eat and then went back to sleep again. But that cat was a hell-raiser in his heyday. No female tabby cat was safe with him around.

So what has that to do with ED, I hear you ask? I would suggest—everything! You see, I believe that lots of males out there get this ED label hung around their necks, until they begin to believe it. Somehow, this fit young virile 50-year-old suddenly gets this disease called ED when in his 60s. Where did this disease come from? Why did he get it? How do you get rid of it, and how do the rest of you make sure you don't get it either?

Before we get too much further into this, I want you to think back to when you were in your late teens, or early 20s. You could run 100 metres in well under 13 seconds. Now you probably can't run that distance at all, let alone clock 13 seconds for it. Is this a new disease? Should we call it 'Leg Dysfunction' or LD for short?

When you were in your 20s, you had no problems reading the newspaper, but by the time you were 40, it was becoming a bit of a problem. By the time you were 60, you really had problems with distance vision as well as reading. We should probably call this 'Visual Dysfunction', but the initials VD have already been taken, so let's call it 'Focusing Dysfunction' or FD for short.

In your 20s you probably didn't have any problems with the erectile thingy either. You know, the dangly bits. In fact, it was probably overactive. But as you got older, the frequency and intensity began to slow up somewhat. By the time you were 60 you were told you had this terrible disease—ED. But what's the difference between LD, FD and ED?

I would suggest to you that there is no difference. I made up LD and FD, because neither is a true 'dysfunction', but just the natural aging that occurs. Likewise, I would suggest that ED is not a true 'dysfunction' when it occurs later in life. It is just part of the natural aging process too. So all you 60 and 70-year-olds (and older) who have been given the label ED, just throw it away. You haven't got a dysfunctional disease. You're just growing older, like my cat.

Now there are a few differences between Mr Tom Cat and Mr Tom Ex-pat. Sex is not just procreative, it is recreational, and is something about which we have built up great mystique. How many emails do you get every day suggesting that you can make the wedding tackle fatter, longer and more active? These days, we judge ourselves on our horizontal achievements, rather than our intellectual achievements. Those with younger wives feel that they are letting the side down (or something else) if they cannot rise to the occasion (sorry about that) every night, or every second night, or every 'whenever' that you have decided 'homework' should be done.

So what should be done about it? Well, first off, Viagra, Cialis and Levitra do work for the majority of the older chaps. However, they open up much more than just the door to the bedroom, they open you up to physical exercise (I was going to say 'viagorous' exercise, but the *Pattaya Mail*'s Ms Hillary used that line first) for which your body might not be fit enough.

This is why these medications should only be taken after examination by a doctor, to ensure your general level of fitness is good enough. Homework shouldn't become work for the undertakers! Dying 'on the job' sort of beats the purpose in my book.

So what should you do? Talk to your doctor and get a good check-up first! If the cardiac fitness is not there, then work on getting the ticker fitter. ED isn't the end of the world. It can be overcome, but do it safely!

And while I think about it, beware of imitations! 'Copy' Viagra is not as good as a copy Rolex. The watch will at least work, while the copy Viagra won't work, while you watch!

~

Healthcare

SOMETIMES IT BECOMES EASY TO forget that you are an alien, living in a foreign land. We *farang*s have an unfortunate tendency to think that we are in an outpost of America, England, Australia or somewhere like that. We have our ex-pat club, we have ex-pat style restaurants supplying English breakfasts, we have English language newspapers, and German ones, and Scandinavian ones, so we are safely cocooned or insulated from the culture of this country. And that is Thai culture, because this is not the USA or the UK, this is Thailand!

Please take careful note of this. This is Amazing Fact Number 1. Thailand is a country with its own unique ways, including language, grammar and even alphabet.

I have to admit that my Thai is very poor. I can feed myself and find a toilet, but not much else. My three-year-old daughter knows more Thai words than I do, and she is now teaching me to read the Thai alphabet.

So far I've mastered *gaw gai*, *kaw kai*, *kaw kuat* and *kaw kwai*, so that's the top line of four, out of the 44, out of the way! I even found out that my own surname starts with *kaw kwai*! I will get there yet, provided I live to around 140.

And by the way, remember that age-old conundrum: 'What came first, the chicken or the egg'? The Thai people have this all worked out, and I can tell you that the correct answer is that the chicken came first. Even my little daughter knows this. *Gaw gai* (for chicken) comes before *kaw kai* (for egg) reading from the left on the top line of the alphabet chart! The chicken comes before the egg! Mystery solved.

However, let us get back to cultural differences and expectations, and there are many, even in the English speaking countries, who theoretically all have the same ways of carrying out health care for their citizens. Is American care different from British care or Australian care? (Other than the fact that Americans can't spell!) The answer is yes, there are great differences in the way medical care is carried out. I was registered in the UK and Australia and have also worked in Europe. I have personal experience to show that health care delivery has many different medical models.

Take the situation of someone going to the doctor with a cough. Not a chronic cough, but one that has gone on for a week. In the US, there will be a battery of tests and X-rays ordered, just to make sure the doctor didn't miss anything because of the ever-present threat of litigation. American lawyers feed on doctors. This will be an expensive cough. The patient pays, not the government.

In Australia, there will be some tests ordered, but these will be limited because the government is watching. Did you know that every three months the doctors in Australia get a printout from the government through the Health Insurance Commission to show how many X-rays, blood tests, etc they have ordered, and compare that number to the national average? Fall outside the median and a man in a suit will be knocking on the surgery door to ask why! So the Aussies will get a medium sized bill for their coughs.

In the UK there will probably be no tests ordered, because the government is paying all the bills. The health system is so overloaded that even if the doctor did order some tests, by the time you actually get the test done, you will either have got better or will have died. So the Brits pay nothing (other than their heavy taxes) and get nothing.

So here are three English speaking countries with three totally different ways of delivering health care to its citizens. Which one is right? All of them? Or none of them?

So when looking dispassionately at health care in Thailand, you should not judge this by your own cultural expectations or experiences. Thailand's medical model is again, like most things Thai, which is to say, different!

Here there is also the duality of public treatment, mainly funded by the government, and private treatment funded by the patient, but underwritten by the medical insurers. This can be complicated, if not properly understood.

Take, for example, the hospital where I work, the Bangkok Hospital Pattaya. This is a fully equipped private hospital, which gets its funding from medical fees. From those medical fees, my hospital spent 1.5 million dollars to bring in the latest state of the art diagnostic equipment for the Radiology department last year, including the 64-Slice CT, just as an example.

Now, down the road at Sattahip is the Queen Sirikit Hospital, which is a Thai government hospital, which also delivers a high standard of Thai style health care, but, it does not have 1.5 million dollars of diagnostic equipment. Governments cannot afford such luxuries.

However, let us move on to health care deliverers and Amazing Fact Number 2. The language spoken by Thai doctors is Thai. This is because they live and work in Thailand, which was Amazing Fact Number 1. Now, the doctors at Bangkok Hospital Pattaya can speak English, but it is obviously not their first language. Why should it be? The majority of the patients they treat are Thai, not ex-pats. However, because there can bé language communication problems when dealing with foreigners, this is but one of the reasons that a consultation with a foreigner takes longer than it does with Thai people. This is hardly an amazing fact, but time is money, even in medicine, so longer consultations will cost more than short consultations. This is the same as in other countries.

Before I leave individual consultations, we have to come back to patient expectations. Having qualified 40 years ago, that makes me not only an old fart, but also means that I've been in the game long enough to see the changes that have occurred in patient expectations in the Western world. My favourite story is the one where the doctor is leaving the house after making a house call and the patient's wife runs out asking, 'Can he eat grapes?' The doctor pauses for a moment, looks wise and says, 'Yes. But only white ones.' Anyone with even the slightest bit of wine knowledge will know it makes zero difference, but in those days, the doctor's words came a close second to the Ten Commandments. They were followed to the letter.

However, over my 40 years of medicine, things have changed. No longer can we get away with the 'only white grapes' routine. Western patients have become too smart, or the doctors relatively more stupid. You have no idea how it makes the doctor cringe when in comes the patient with 200 sheets of computer printouts under his or her arm. The Internet is a great thing, but few people check the information you can get on it for accuracy.

Consultations now become a battleground where the doctor has to convince the patient of the diagnosis, which may be quite different from what the patient thinks he's got, with his 200 page printouts. Even when consensus has been reached as far as diagnosis is concerned, there then comes the treatment to be ordered. The Western patient expects to be consulted as to what medications he or she will have to take, what the side effects are, if various drugs be combined and will it work with Echinacea, or this month's magic health herb.

Now, note that scenario is what happens with the Western patient. The Thai patient is quite different. Thais still believe every word the doctor says—'Yes, white grapes are fine'—and do not question the diagnosis or treatment in any way. In fact, they may not even be given the diagnosis, but that doesn't matter. Thai patients also have the expectation that they will be given a big bag of tablets at the end. This is to get their money's worth from the consultation.

So now perhaps you can see why a Thai doctor will also give you a large bag of goodies every time as well. The Thai doctor, practising in Thailand, does what he has been trained to do, to fulfil the expectations of Thai patients. There are those *farang*s who believe that the number of tablets is just to sell more drugs and pay for new buildings. It is not. It is to satisfy the Thai expectations.

So what can you do about it? My advice is to find a doctor you like and train your chosen physician in your expectations. Be prepared to ask questions as to what medications you are going to be given. Be prepared to say, 'I don't need any paracetamol as I have plenty of them at home.'

And this is as good a time as ever to introduce Amazing Fact Number 3. All drugs are not necessarily the same. Just the same way as you can get a copy Polo shirt, a copy Rolex and a copy Gucci handbag, you can also get copy blood pressure medication and even a copy of Vitamin V, otherwise known as Viagra, the Patron Saint of sexagenarians. That means people in their 60s, not what you thought immediately! Copy medicines are definitely cheaper, because the drug companies making them are not paying royalties to manufacture a patented drug. Drugs that the parent manufacturers have spent millions of dollars to produce, which has to be recouped, so naturally the price of the genuine article is more than the copy.

The other fact to remember is called bioavailability. I'll talk about Viagra again, not that any of you strapping young chaps reading this book will ever need it. The chemical in Viagra is Sildenafil, and the chemical in the copy blue tablet is also Sindenafil. So they are the same. Right? Wrong!

The matrix of the tablet can affect the rate of absorption of the Sildenafil, so one works by the time you have walked up the stairs, while the other will have you sitting around playing Whistling Dixie for a couple of hours before the blood levels are high enough. This is called the bioavailability factor.

So, what are the hospitals like in Thailand? It may interest you to know that my eldest son is also a doctor, practising in Australia, and he comes over every year to visit his little sister and young brother. He has toured my hospital here, and his words? 'Dad, we've got nothing like this in Australia!' And there are even more hospitals like mine in the private arena in Thailand.

So Thailand has the expertise, it has the cutting edge technology, there is no waiting list, and it is cheaper than the private sector in the West. Let me know when you're coming over and I'll book a bed for you!

~

Jumping Without a Safety Net

MOST EX-PATS HAVE COME FROM a country that has some form of government healthcare. All our lives we have grown up with that medical safety net to look after us in times of medical problems. Call it the National Health, or Medicare, it makes sure you won't be left stranded. Certainly, your taxes are being used to look after you, and public hospital treatment can be maddeningly slow with waiting lists measured in years and not months. But it is there.

Now comes Thailand, and for many ex-pats in their first year, they blissfully carry on, imagining that there is this medical back-up system that will help them. But there isn't.

The Thai public hospital system is for Thais. Not for *farang*s. Especially not for those *farang*s who have retired and are not paying any Thai taxes. After all, a Thai cannot use the British NHS, even when married to an English person. They have to see someone privately.

So it comes as a very rude shock to the new ex-pat to find that he is required to visit a private hospital with his ailments, and as the average ex-pat is older, ailments become even more prevalent. And private hospitals are a business, and payment at the point of service is required.

Comparatively, medical costs in the private sector in Thailand are much less than the costs in the West. This is one reason for medical tourism to Thailand. However, treatment is still a cost that must be met. As I said, there is no safety net here.

The answer, of course, is private medical insurance. This is another minefield for the *farang* to traverse. There are so many health plans. Which is the best? And then what company? Should you stick with an insurance company whose name you recognise from the 'old country'? Or plump for a local company you have never heard of?

It is too far removed from the concept of this book for me to advise you on what way to go—that is the province of the insurance agent, not the scribbling medico. But I would advise against going directly to the insurance company to take out your policy. Why? Because if there is a difference in opinion between yourself and your insurer, who is going to go to bat for you? The insurance company certainly is not, is it? Again that is like asking your estranged wife's solicitor to act on your behalf as well in a messy divorce.

The next question; is your insurance cover enough? This is a perennial problem. And a perennial headache for private hospitals and those who end up in them! And if you haven't upgraded your cover recently, then you may be in for a nasty surprise.

Unfortunately, everything, be that petrol, bread, or baby's nappies has gone up in price in the past 12 months. If you haven't upgraded there could be a shortfall, which you would have to find (or fund), not your insurance company.

At the outset, I must say I have never been one out of whom insurance agents grow fat. It has always been my feeling that there was something unbalanced about my attendant hangers on (aka children) getting rich at my expense when I meet my final demise. When you really analyse it, you don't even get to enjoy your own wake! No, if anyone is going to benefit from my paying insurance premiums every year, it is going to be me!

I have also been very lucky with my choice of careers. Being a medico does have advantages. If I couldn't fix my skin rash or whatever, I could always ring a classmate who could (or should) be able to. Medications and drugs? Again no worries, just a quick raid of the samples cupboard in my surgery and I had everything I needed.

What about Hospital in-patient insurance? I passed on that one too. After all, the only foreseeable problems that could stop me working were massive trauma following a road accident or suchlike, or a heart attack. In either case you don't care where you are as long as there are wall to wall running doctors and plenty of painkillers. In Australia, the 'free' public hospital system is fine for that.

So I blithely carried on through life insuranceless. I did spend one night in hospital with a broken leg 30 years ago, so as regards personal medical costs versus proposed insurance premiums, I was still miles in front.

And then I came to Thailand. Still I blithely carried on. After all, I was ten foot tall and bulletproof. Then a friend over here had a stroke and required hospitalisation. Said friend was four years younger than me and I was forced to review the ten foot bulletproof situation, only to find that I was actually only five foot eleven and my anti-kryptonite had expired.

Thailand was a completely new ball game. Enquiries as to hospital and medical costs showed that they were considerably less than the equivalent in Oz, but, and here's the big but, there's no government system or sickness benefits to fall back on. Suddenly you are walking the tightrope and there's no safety net to stop you hitting terra firma.

So I took out medical insurance. Still it was no gold plated cover. But it was enough to look after me if I needed hospitalisation, and that came sooner than I imagined. I had always subscribed to the 'major trauma' theory, but two days of the galloping gut-rot had me flat on my back with the IV tube being my only lifeline to the world. We are only mortal—even us medicos.

Do you have medical insurance? Perhaps it is time to chat to a reputable insurance agent! Yes, reliable insurance agents and reliable insurance companies do exist, but you need help through the minefield.

You also need help when it comes to filling out the application forms, in my opinion. And you also need to be 100% truthful. Yes, insurance companies will check on your records, and if it is found that you have been sparing with the truth over pre-existing conditions, expect a shock at settling up time at the cashier's desk.

Remember too, that just because you have an insurance card does not automatically signify that 'everything' is covered. This is why private hospitals will ask you for a deposit on admission. If the insurance company later verify that you are indeed covered for that ailment or condition, then you'll get it back, but you have to prove that you are covered, not the other way round!

And remember that cheap insurance premiums really just means you are only getting partial cover. A point to ponder. Medical bills in Thailand can easily reach one million baht these days, so make sure you have enough cover. My friendly insurance agent also tells me that if you take out five million baht cover, he can arrange resurrection! But don't believe him.

~

Why the Brits Live Here

THE QUICKEST WAY TO REALLY appreciate just why we all came to live in Thailand is called a 'trip back home'. For me, 'home' is with my wife and children in Jomtien, but my passport says that I am a UK citizen. From the authority's point of view, that's where my home is, and I'm probably stuck with it.

Once a year, we make the trek back to the north of Scotland to visit Mother, a hale and hearty 88-year-old widow, if one ignores the fact that she has macular degeneration making her legally blind. A few years ago, as Mother had still not seen our baby daughter (literally or figuratively), we decided we would make the trip, complete with then-13-month-old Marisa.

In retrospect, in the annals of 'smart moves', this decision, on a scale of 1-10 of smart moves, would rate around a strong 0.05.

We were appraised of this fact, less than 30 minutes into the skies from Bangkok, as Miss Marisa emptied

the contents of her stomach all over the back of my
wife's seat. Really rubbing in the lack of wisdom in
this move was the total lack of help, or even sympathy,
from the trolley dollies in our 747, as we mopped and
scrubbed and wiped down their seat. Finally I just asked
for another blanket which we used as a sponge. (If you
fly via a Far East airline, avoid seat number 36 E. You
have been warned!)

With more than a faint odour surrounding us, we
finally made Aberdeen in the north of Bonnie Scotland.
The immigration people were very nice, and quick, but
of course this could have been through the olfactory
factor too.

Through the wonders of modern aviation, we had
left Bangkok airport at 2am and a balmy 34 degrees
Celsius, to walk out into the balmy climes of Northern
Scotland's 5.5 degrees at 3pm, their time. Forget jet lag
and culture shock. This was Centigrade shock. And,
oh yes, it was raining. The rain that the British Isles is
famous for. The wet stuff leaves the clouds, but doesn't
really make it to the ground, it just hangs there. And
of course it pervades everything, so that by the time
we found the hire car in the car park we were enjoying
wet clothes, clinging to our bodies at the 5.5 degrees of
Scotland's spring.

'Home' was then only another two hours by road,
noting every couple of miles that there was yet another
sign, advising me that speed cameras were in operation,
up hill, down dale or on the flat. I got the feeling that the
police considered me a dangerous auto-criminal, or at

least I felt that way. Welcome to paranoia! Population: Just you!

The next day, rather than cook, we decided to eat out at the local pub for a counter lunch. I swallowed hard as I read the large print covering budget eats, to see that a baguette was on offer for a mere (Sterling converted to Thai) 450 baht. Three of those and a beer and 2,000 baht went past the tonsils, never to be reclaimed, in any usable form at least!

The following day I donned several overcoats, erected an umbrella, and braved the five degrees ambient to the safety of the car, and with wipers ablaze (it was still raining) made it to the petrol station, where I waited expectantly at the pumps. If it had not been for other motorists getting their own gasoline and giving me the nod, I might still be there, cold and perfectly preserved like the mastodon they found in the ice in Russia. (It might have been waiting for a McMastodon Meal, you never know.)

Moving smartly to avoid exposure to the cold I put 30 litres in the tank by myself and ran to the pay window, where the nice young lady with the red cheeks and Scottish brogue informed me that my purchase cost £26.70. For those without the instant currency converter that's a tad shy of 20,000 baht, or more simply, around 66 baht a litre for unleaded petrol. I decided that the police did not need speed cameras, just a reminder that if you put your foot down, it uses more petrol!

After two weeks it was time for the tearful farewells, except for the fact that my tear ducts were frozen over, so we hightailed it to the airport. For the flight home (or back to Thailand if you want to be pedantic), we were again regaled by Miss Marisa deciding to throw up in the plane. This time, rather than her mother's seat, she chose the feet of the poor unfortunate sod who had scored seat 36 F. (Further note for those contemplating flying on an airline from the Far East, avoid both 36 E and 36 F. You have been warned—twice!)

Perhaps I do the UK an injustice. Many people do live (read 'exist') there, so it can't be all that bad, other than the climate, the price of everything, and the all pervading speed cameras. It comes as no shock to me to see the number of British ex-pat pensioners in Thailand, who can live like veritable kings in this Kingdom on their meagre pensions.

We stepped out into the Bangkok sunshine and drove home to Jomtien in our air-conditioned car, happily paying the 22-something baht for a litre of gasoline. With no speed cameras to record our progress, we made it home without paranoia and frequent references to the speedometer. Rather than cook when we got back, I bought a baguette with filling for 85 baht and laughed all the way to the lunch table.

However, don't get me wrong. The UK's a great place—to leave from!

~

Medical Tourism

THE WESTERN WORLD IS BECOMING increasingly aware of the presence of Thailand as a tourist destination. In the English and European language speaking countries, visitors from the UK (540,401), the US (465, 135), Germany (324,616) and Aussies (301,767) arrived in Thailand between January and October 2006—an increase over the same period in the previous year. (Figures supplied by the Immigration Bureau, Royal Thai Police Department.)

Some of the increased numbers coming to Thailand in that quoted period were not the usual tourists, but were in fact medical tourists, the human components of one of the fastest growing sectors of international tourism.

Ten years ago, medical tourism was hardly known. One decade later, more than 250,000 patients per year visit Singapore alone—nearly half of them from the Middle East. This year, approximately half a million foreign patients will travel to India for medical care, while four years ago, the number was only 150,000.

In financial terms, experts estimate that medical tourism could bring India as much as US$ 2.2 billion per year by 2012. Argentina, Costa Rica, Cuba, Jamaica, South Africa, Jordan, Malaysia, Hungary, Latvia and Estonia have their hands up, trying to break into this lucrative market. In Thailand, we are already one of the major destinations and we know that medical tourism will bring in US$ 1 billion to this country this year. A sizable sum, and one that should not be ignored.

Of course, this prompts the question: Why would anyone from the West risk going overseas to have their surgery? Especially for procedures that they can have done at home? One of the principal reasons is cost. Medical and dental treatment in Asia costs far less than the similar procedure in Australia. In fact, many Australians, Americans and Brits simply cannot afford private health care costs, or even the insurance premiums.

There is also another reason for the increasing numbers of medical tourists: An increasingly aging population. By 2015, the health of the vast Baby Boomer generation will have begun to deteriorate. With more than 220 million Boomers in the United States, Canada, Europe, Australia and New Zealand, this represents a significant market looking for high-quality medical care.

And what do they come for? The major attractions are cosmetic surgery and dental treatments. However, eye surgery, kidney dialysis and organ transplantation are also among common procedures sought by medical vacationers to Thailand. We even have a number of tourists coming for sex change operations, with Thai surgeons being amongst the leaders in this field. Not quite what you might expect from the macho countries in the West, but understandable procedures for a small, but troubled patient group.

In the Western world, cosmetic surgery is not covered by the national medical insurance schemes such as the NHS in the UK or the Australian or American Medicare schemes. If you want a new nose or bouncing boobs, then you personally will have to meet the bill. Your health insurance will not.

However, there are other medical tourists, not just those wishing to change their appearance, or their sex. These are the people who require non-urgent elective surgery. This group includes hip and knee replacements, heart surgery and vascular operations, as well as some eye operations, all of which can be covered by national health insurance schemes, but are subject to long waiting lists! We are told that the only way some patients move up the waiting list overseas is when those higher up the line die before getting to the operating table! This has become so much of a problem in some States in Australia that there are moves afoot to try and lessen the backlog of patients from the waiting list, by getting Medicare to fund the cost of the overseas operations. Government sponsored medical tourism!

Returning to the 'cost' factor; how much cheaper is it to have procedures carried out in Thailand, compared to other countries? The following is one example—and this is one taken directly from my own files—featuring a young couple from Australia who came for a 10 day holiday to Thailand, with time spent in the usual three tourist destinations of Bangkok, Phuket and Pattaya. While here in Pattaya, the woman also had the LASIK laser procedure done to both eyes at the Bangkok Hospital Pattaya. The holiday here for both of them, including air fares and accommodation, plus the surgery for her, cost less than the fee for the LASIK operation alone in Australia.

Another example, and one of the more common cosmetic procedures that is carried out in Thailand, is breast augmentation. I believe the usual charge in Australia is now around AU$ 12,000, while the entire procedure here, again including operations, fares, trips, transfers, etc, will cost less than half that. 'That certainly was a great holiday you had in Thailand, Sheila. You look so much better!' And only she (and her cosmetic surgeon) really knows why!

And again from our records, coming to see the tooth fairy is top of the list of procedures asked for, and then there were almost 7,000 people who came to the Beauty Centre for cosmetic reasons. In fact, when you look at patients by nationality, foreigners make up 41% of our patients, and just over half of those were tourists.

Since medical tourism is such an important part of the hospital's income, we have not been sitting on our hands, hoping westerners will walk in the door, looking for big ticket items. We have found that the medical tourist wants:

- Quality
- Service
- Price
- and Destination.

Looking at these factors, the patients demand Quality of medical care, and this is demonstrated through internationally recognised accreditation. This is where Thailand's hospitals competing in the medical tourism marketplace have to ensure they really are of international standard. ISO certification is a must, which we have had in Pattaya for some years, and we are even in the process of receiving accreditation through the American Joint Commission International Accreditation organisation (JCIA). In medicine, our standards have to be undeniably demonstrated for overseas visitors to have enough faith to place their lives in the care of 'foreign' doctors.

Towards this end, for example, we have gained international awards for not only the hospital, but also for the procedures carried out by the hospital surgeons, such as the SuperSight Surgery, in which we are amongst the world leaders. Incidentally, I believe this new form of eye surgery, which implants focusable intra-ocular lenses has yet to reach many countries in the West!

The doctors in our hospital have been chosen, in all the different specialties, because of their expertise—and an ability to communicate with international patients in

English. Many in fact have trained or worked overseas themselves. To help them, the hospital employs me, as an English speaking doctor, with part of my brief being to assist the Thai doctors in the English languages. To know there is a 'friendly white face' on the staff certainly takes much apprehension away from the foreign medical tourists!

Thailand is also getting a name for itself with the advances being done in Stem Cell therapy. Whilst there are problems with this being given the green light overseas, terminal patients are more than willing to give anything a shot. And Thailand has the medical infrastructure, and now, the expertise as well, in this somewhat controversial therapy.

Also intimately tied to Quality is the actual hospital itself. In this year alone, we have continued to develop the hospital where I work and have opened our fifth wing complete with helipad, providing another 200 beds, with many of the private room floors dedicated solely to our international patients. There is also a dedicated International Medical Centre, which is set up purely for tourists.

Since patients in Thailand do come from all over the world, good communication is then a must between the hospitals and the medical tourists, and in my hospital we cover 22 languages spoken by the staff of the International Department. Being able to have queries answered by staff fluent in the language and understanding questions goes a long way towards getting selection of the hospital by the medical tourist.

Service is, of course, one area where Thailand has a wonderful reputation. As a nation, Thai people are known as being a caring race. Put a caring person in a caring profession and I say you literally get a double dose of care, and for the medical tourist, they get that in the hospital environment.

As far as an attractive destination is concerned, the Tourism Authority of Thailand has done a fine job in promoting this country as a superb place for a holiday (and some of us, like me, are lucky enough to live here permanently)!

Medical Tourism will continue to grow while there is such a price differential. I believe the benefits outweigh the risks, and medical tourism has opened up new possibilities for many people in the West who otherwise could not afford to have their surgery in their homeland.

So you can see the attraction of coming over. And you'll see it even better if you get your eyes done here too!

~

Getting Into the House

THINK BACK TO WHEN YOU moved into your first home. An exciting time for both you and your partner. Those of you of a romantic nature probably even picked up your bride and carried her over the threshold. Ah yes, there is a spark of humanity still evident in the Western breast (or was that 'beast').

So is living in Thailand any different? Yes, in every way possible, especially when it comes to things such as houses. You must never forget that Thai people are exceptionally superstitious. Houses are built on the ground, and the ground is run by its own teams of spirits.

But I get a little in front of myself. If you have read the chapter on getting house loans, then yes, we finally did get a loan to buy the house we had chosen (read 'my wife' had chosen) as the ideal place to bring up our children. I have to admit, a brand new, three bedroom, two bathroom, lounge, dining room and kitchen with a reasonable sized piece of dirt for 2,000,000 baht (around £30,000 sterling) was certainly not expensive.

We waited for the completion, going round as all new house owners do every weekend to check on the progress and tell the builders unimportant details, including the fact that we expected the kitchen to at least have a tap that delivered water. Much in Thailand must not just be left to common sense. A goodly amount of double-checking goes a long way.

Finally the three bed, two bath bungalow was finished, to the builder's satisfaction, if not ours, and we began to make plans to shift from our then current abode.

For me, this was a case of taking up a mate's offer in the removals business, and a date was fixed for the following Friday. I proudly told my wife of the arrangements, pleased to show her the 'farang connection' worked well in this country called Thailand. She was pleased that the furniture would be shifted, but there was a problem.

'What's wrong?' I asked.

Of course it was the fact that the next Friday was not the auspicious day to move into the new house. It was the next Wednesday. Silly me, forgetting such important facts. Apparently the fortune teller or other such geomancer had been consulted and it was definitely Wednesday, and we would have to perform a small ceremony as well.

I agreed and said that after the ceremonial Wednesday we would then move in fully on the Friday. Not quite so easy. For the ceremony to be fully able to prepare the house for the invasion of my wife, nanny, two children and the *farang*, we had to sleep there as well that evening. Again I felt this was no great imposition, as we could bring over the mattresses ourselves and complete our end of the appeasing the spirits bargain, then return to the old house, ready for the Friday move.

Not quite so easy either, I was told. Once we have the ceremony, we should stay there till the Friday and furniture came around. I agreed wholeheartedly (any person married to a Thai reading this book will understand just how easy this makes your life, especially when you have really no idea of what is going on!)

So it was arranged. The ceremony would be Wednesday.

'How long will it take?' said the novice new house-occupier-to-be.

'Maybe an hour,' was the reply.

'So I'll take an hour off work,' said I.

'Better you take the morning off,' was the reply. I could see there were parts of this ceremony that were not going to be fully revealed before the fateful morning. *Was it sacrificial pigs this time*, I wondered inwardly. I let them know at the hospital that I wouldn't be in on the Wednesday morning. When I said it was for the new house ceremony they all appeared to know immediately and agreed that it would take all morning.

Wednesday rolled around and the preparations began early morning at the old abode. Candles, Buddha statues and other paraphernalia appeared from secret hiding places and we were all made ready, including the cat.

'Do we have to bring the cat?'

'Yes, everybody who will live in the new house has to be there.'

So we loaded the car with strange ceremonial objects, the happy family and an unhappy cat. But there was a slight matter of having to talk to the spirits of the ground, living in the spirit houses of the old house. They were invited to follow us to the new house as well. How the incumbent spirits were going to take this invasion by the old lot I had no idea, but when it comes to things Thai, I generally have no idea. 'The more you know, the less you understand,' is a dictum which contains the everlasting truth for foreigners living here. We all smile to ourselves listening to some visitor expounding Thai wisdom to his equally as inexperienced mates in any bar. If only they knew!

We arrived at the new house, by now having also picked up my wife's cousin and the village guard who was also standing by. How she knew we were coming I do not know either, but perhaps she got the nod from the expectant spirits.

Now we were marshalled into a line, each carrying semi-sacred objects, and myself with an oil lamp.

'Walk three times round the house,' was the command and away we went. Me (with a lighter to re-ignite the wick which kept on blowing out), wife (with two Buddha images), nanny, cousin, Marisa, Evan, security guard and the even more unhappy cat.

After the third tour we entered the house, where a small altar had been prepared for the Buddha images, candles lit for the lustral water and a bowl with rice and money mixed together. All those with Thai ID cards then intoned a reverie, while the *farang* looked at the floor and the children picked each other's noses.

And so it ended. The cat bolted and I made returning to work noises. But it wasn't going to be that easy. By now you know that nothing in Thailand ever is 'that' easy. There was the small matter of the central pillar.

Central pillars are important. Every Thai township has one. Every Thai building has one—and so did ours—and it was going to get its due quota of respect as well. My wife brought out some lengths of red, white and yellow material which contained many strange herbs and other items which could have been ceremonial finger amputations for all I knew.

'I brought this from my village,' said my wife, as if that would make it more understandable.

Standing on two chairs, I was instructed to tightly wrap the rolled-up cloths around the pole closest to the centre of the house, such that they and their contents would stay up there. This took both of us, tugging and grunting with an end each, knotting them together, and then leafy branches were inserted between the cloth and the pillar.

And so it was over. The house spirits were appeased. The old lot and the new lot came to an agreement, the security guard was given a bottle of beer and the cat had disappeared. But we were in. Even if the cat wasn't.

On the Friday, the AGS Four Winds removal people brought over the furniture and four weeks later I finally located most of my belongings. Of course I could have just asked the spirits of the house to find them for me, but I was unsure of how and where and to whom to phrase the request. It is simpler to ask my three-year-old daughter. She seems to know everything these days, and being half Thai means that she has much more chance of knowing these things than I!

By the way, the cat returned ten days later.

~

Chaiyapruek Road and the Saga of the Drains

I LIVE IN CHAIYAPRUEK ROAD in Jomtien, on the Eastern Seaboard of Thailand. It is a fairly ordinary kind of street, made of concrete poured in four lane sections, so there is room to park either side, and two lanes in the middle for the traffic to run unimpeded in both directions.

A few years ago we were woken up early in the morning with the sounds of an incessant 'thump-thump' somewhere outside. Staggering outside, I was visually and aurally assaulted by a large yellow road machine, fitted with a vertical battering ram that was systematically cracking the concrete surface of the road. And right outside my house. Looking further down the road there were two large bulldozers, plus a huge scooping machine, steadily ripping up my street.

Since my command of the Thai language is enough to feed me and find toilets, my wife was sent forth to find out what was happening. She returned with news, none of which was good. Our road was scheduled for upgrading, and new drainage pipes would be laid. The process would be completed by July. Considering that this was early March, it looked as if vehicular access for the next four months could present a few problems. 'A few problems,' became the understatement of 2004.

Very quickly the team of voracious road machines dug up the concrete roadway, but they did leave one lane untouched, on the opposite side from my gateway. Of course this meant that over a 500 metre stretch of Chaiyapruek there was single vehicle one-way access, but vehicles would attack from both ends, with the inevitable Mexican stand-off in the middle.

With no 'Right of Way' it became a 'Right of Weight' situation. Might became right. The family Daihatsu Mira did not do too well in these encounters. I took to parking in a nearby village and tramping through the diggings, morning and evening. Muddy feet became the rule of the day. My wife suggested I leave one clean pair of shoes in the car, and retain the claggy, mucky pair for the daily mountaineering assault course.

I became used to coming home to see a totally different terrain. Sometimes there was a deep ditch outside my gate, on others a giant earthen hill. Then a long three metre deep trench was dug and a concrete sectioned drain arrived. I could no longer even see my house and had to gain access to my gate by walking along the fences of my neighbours. But worse was yet to come!

The first 'worse' was when they cut through the water pipes leading to the house. This they managed to do very successfully, every day for two weeks. Someone in charge of a ditch digger was a slow learner.

The next 'worse' was when they managed to cut the overhead electric power lines with the arm of the excavator. Now we had neither power, nor water. We began to assume a siege mentality.

Then they dug up the entrance to the village where I would park in the evenings. The closest I could now get was to park on the dirt road behind my house, and with a machete, hack a pathway to my back door through the verdant tropical jungle of the vacant allotments.

My wife came to the rescue, and with 500 baht she managed to get one of the bulldozers to trundle round behind our house and cut a swathe through the aforementioned verdant tropicality, and I was able to stop carrying a machete and snake stick in the car, along with the spare pair of shoes.

From the vantage point of my front veranda I was able to witness the laying to rest of the concrete drain, and its covering with the mound of dirt outside my gate. It was a bizarre scene, akin to that wonderful cult movie *Harold and Maude*, whose principal characters met in cemeteries. I smiled again, knowing that the end was in sight. Silly *farang* me!

No sooner was one pipe down when they came along and excavated another trench right beside the first one! This time, instead of a concrete square section drain, we were to get a concrete circular section drain as well.

The earth was no sooner packed down over drain two, when they came along and excavated a third trench for the large black plastic pipe of drain number three. This had to be the end!

Not yet, young man. We now dug up and uncovered drain number one, to feed in several blue plastic drains from what was left of the footpath. But I could see they were running out of drains. The siege would soon be over.

Concrete trucks arrived, concrete was poured, Chaiyapruek looked like a road again, and I could even sometimes get to within 50 metres of my front gate. Shopping was no longer an exercise in trudging through the jungle with plastic bags. It was (almost) bliss. But they were not finished yet!

Back came the jackhammers and they drilled through the road and into the top of the drains, making holes for inspection covers and grates. About every three metres. Nice round holes were boxed up and more concrete was poured. Surely this would be it? After all, it was now October and seven months. Not so fast again! The manhole covers seemed to be in short supply.

So now, at the time of writing, I can do a slalom down Chaiyapruek Road, avoiding the oncoming traffic that is doing its own evasive action around poorly indicated holes in the road, that other vehicles fall into very regularly (and my wife at the helm of the Mira once). There are probably even a couple of bicycles and the odd street dog that has come to grief, but as we enter November we can look forward to driving unimpeded down the best drained street in Thailand. My street, my Thailand.

~

Living Through My First Coup

ON 19 SEPTEMBER I FOUND I could add another exploit to my list that I will take with me to the pearly gates. I lived through a military coup d'etat!

There I was, a stout stick at the ready, sitting in my foxhole with my tin hat on as the shells whistled over my head. Well, that is what everyone outside of Thailand seemed to think, the next few days being flurries of phone calls from concerned relatives and friends from all over the world. However, that little scenario could not have been further from the truth.

It was a Tuesday morning and as I drove to the hospital I was smiling, as I was having such a good run through the traffic. In fact there seemed to be fewer cars than normal, but there was nothing so untoward that it might have raised my suspicions.

My first port of call in the morning is the Doctor's Lounge, where we are given a buffet breakfast and newspapers to read, and I was looking forward to it, as

Tuesdays are '*moo ping*'—a type of BBQ skewered pork that I enjoy.

Opening the door, there were the usual bunch of early birds, but no papers and no *moo ping*.

'Where's the papers?' I asked.

'No news is good news,' replied the gastro-enterologist. I still did not grasp the significance. Then came a bulletin on the TV, and they all rushed to view the scene of some severe faced army, navy and air force officers sitting in a row, while one read a prepared speech. My Thai is not good enough to handle TV bulletins, so I asked what was happening.

'There's been a coup,' said the neurologist.

'What does this mean for us?' I asked.

'Nothing,' said the radiologist, 'it's the way we change governments we don't like,' he said.

The papers arrived late, with words like 'COUP' in banner headlines and photographs inside of people giving roses to the army tank commanders and placing yellow ribbons around the tank gun barrels. Never mind tying yellow ribbons around the 'old oak tree', we had tank gun barrels instead.

And so the first day of the new regime rolled on. And the tanks rolled out, leaving just a few so that holidaymakers could be photographed with a tank in Bangkok. It gave them something to do, because the first edict from the coup leaders had been to declare a public holiday, which was why there was less traffic than usual.

Now how the populace knew about the holiday so quickly, I do not know. It seems that only the deposed prime minister Thaksin Shinawatra and I were unaware of the coup. However, I was not going to feel quite as slighted as he.

Of course, the embassies were immediately hotbeds of misinformation, with the Americans first off the mark with their blanket travel warnings. The Australians, leading from behind as usual, were next. Newspapers like the *News of the World* were full of reports of tourists panicking and rushing to leave the nation's capital, Bangkok. 'Never let the truth get in the way of a good story' has been a newspaper dictum for aeons, and the salacious press was having a field day with their reports of terror and panic.

Meanwhile all those tourists who didn't read the *News of the World* were still happily posing with the remaining tanks as the coup rolled on to Day Two.

By this stage, the local banner headlines were saying 'Bloodless Coup!' which indeed it was. After the public holiday, life was much the same as before, the traffic was just as bad and tourists came and left as usual. The hospital had its normal influx of patients each morning and the usual discharges in the afternoons. The only change was that the deposed, now ex-PM, was photographed alone and lonely in London, and nobody cared, despite the millions he had accumulated during his five years in office.

Within a very short period of time, an interim government was appointed, the members of the previous ruling party defected in droves, and it was completely back to normal.

I had survived my first coup d'etat, but never even saw a tank. I feel cheated somewhat. Surely they could have dropped a tank in Pattaya for the tourists to photograph. Thailand missed another tourism photo opportunity, I am sorry to say.

I have put my tin hat away for a more appropriate time. By the way, the reference to stout sticks was one of historical significance. My mother is still in possession of the directive from the Home Office in the UK in WWII which instructed the members of the Home Guard that in case of invasion 'officers should arm themselves with stout sticks!'

Dear me, if Herr Shickelgruber, or Hitler to most of us, only knew, we would all have been speaking German by now!

~

Dancing with a Drag Queen

No overview of Thailand, no matter how brief, would be complete without a mention of the '*katoey*' in the make-up of the nation. And make-up is probably the operative word. It is a sobering thought for all the testosterone-fuelled lads who come to visit Thailand, that the best looking women are always men. Sad in some ways, but true and (almost) understandable.

Books and scientific papers have been written about this group in Thai society, and I believe there is another on the way from Maverick House itself, but the subject is so complex that it would be difficult to completely cover it all in a paperback. Do not forget that Thailand is one of the few countries in the world to have three official sex classifications—men, women and women of the 2nd category. I believe that Brazil has a similar situation and the Carnaval brings them out en masse (correct spelling for the annual celebration, by the way, as it comes from the native-spoken Portuguese).

Unfortunately, in Thailand, '*katoey*' covers many in the gender mix. There are transvestites, transsexuals, cross-dressers, drag queens and female impersonators. There are probably even more. They are all different in degree and it would be wrong to think of them all as the same. Female impersonators such as Danny La Rue, or even Pattaya's Dwee (Malibu's Tina Turner), dress as males in between performances. They are actors.

Transvestites and cross-dressers tend to be variants of the same basic mindset. They are males who enjoy dressing as women, but think of themselves as men. They may be homosexual, or bisexual, or in it for the money. Who would know in Thailand?

Transsexuals are the smallest group, and these are really the classic one sex in the body of another sex. Usually these are females trapped in a male body. I interviewed one such lady (and believe me, she was a lady in all respects, and I don't just mean the missing dangly bits) and she told me she had known she was a female since the age of six. Life had been hard for her. She had even worked as a storeman, though she was much smaller than the other male workers, saving her money to come to Pattaya to try for work in one of Pattaya's famous transvestite shows. She was successful, saved more money and had the total gender reassignment surgery carried out. She had no regrets, she informed me; she was just sad that she could not have children of her own.

I have watched her on stage, calling up the children in the audience to dance with her. She has true maternal urges. She is a woman, even if at one stage she was considered a man. For these people—and we should never forget that *katoeys* are 'people' too—their 'natural attraction' is towards males (as they are females mentally). This means that they are actually heterosexual, and not homosexual. An interesting point for you to ponder.

It should also be understood that many transsexuals hold down ordinary jobs (as women)— they are not all entertainers—so you do not instantly recognise these people at all. However, they are almost always beautifully made up. Pansit Sukarom, aka Pok, a noted *katoey* make-up artist, was quoted in *The Nation* newspaper as saying, 'I used to dress in line with the transsexual's long-standing motto: "Long hair is the diamond crown for all transsexuals." Every feature from head to toe—like the face, breasts, hair and hips—must look perfect (from surgery), so that real women can't compete.'

I did see one of these stunningly beautiful women one night, and could not keep my eyes off her. Breathtakingly immaculate. Her male companion saw my less than furtive stares and turned to me and said, 'I know she's a *katoey*, but she's the best woman I've ever been with. We have been together for seven years.' Another point to ponder.

The *katoey* performers are an interesting and generally fun-loving group. When I was coming up to my 57th birthday, I was searching for a suitable venue. For me, this was going to be a significant occasion—no male in my family had ever seen his 57th birthday, my father suddenly popping his clogs two weeks short, and he had held the longevity record up till then.

So where should this momentous occasion be held? Answer—on stage at the Malibu Cabaret surrounded by *katoey*s. No member of my family had ever done that! The birthday was an outrageous success and one in which the editor of the *Pattaya Mail* presented me with an apron featuring large protuberant rubber breasts, in which I was photographed for posterity. Did this then make me a cross-dresser? Apparently not. I have not worn said apron since.

The *katoey* is an integral part of Thai society, and there have been many who have attempted to work out why. Is it a genetic defect? A societal role needed by a strict Thai sexual society? Or just a bunch of people allowed to be themselves? The answer to these questions is well outside the scope of this book, but I passed by a stand in the Royal Garden Plaza the other day, and there for sale were 'Silicone buttocks'! These I presume would be a 'must have' accessory for the novice *katoey*. I did not add them to my shopping list!

However, just where does the drag queen come in? Let me tell you. I was at a function one evening and spotted this amazing creature outfitted in a black dress, slashed to the waist with brief hot pants underneath, with a huge mop-head of curly hair. It was so over the top, I had to ask her for a dance. In the middle of the dance floor I embarrassedly asked, 'Are you a *katoey*?'

She stopped, fixed me with a steely gaze and said in a most affronted tone of voice, 'No! I'm not a *katoey*! I'm a drag queen.'

At that point I thought to myself, 'I've done it all. I've just danced with a drag queen.'

And that's enough from me on that subject.

~

A *katoey*, or ladyboy; one of the many diverse types to be found in a country where there are actually three recognised genders—males, females, and females of the second kind.

Terminally Late

SOME OF MY RESPONSIBILITIES REQUIRE me to frequently travel to the north of Thailand. While I might prefer not to deliver my un-embalmed body to a faceless voice at the sharp end of a plane, 'This is your captain speaking, we are now cruising at 33,000 feet ...' a height at which, if I jump, will take me several minutes to find terra firma, painfully and terminally, I am stuck with it. This height is also three times higher than that from which I have jumped out of a plane before, but I did have a parachute. Big difference.

Have you noticed that none of the carriers, full price, cut price or slashed price offer you a parachute? No, they insist you wear a lap belt to keep you in the plane until it touches ground and has stopped. The nice lady in the uniform even instructs you in this, whilst at the same time telling you that if you turn on your mobile phone before the plane has stopped at the terminal, dreadful things will happen and the pilot will lose his way. While taxiing towards the terminal, I find this rather amazing, but then, I've never been a pilot; I have only been a passenger.

Really, the only guarantee that the airlines give you, their passenger, is that you will be returned to mother earth. 100% guarantee. I have never read about a plane staying up there forever. I have also studied the safety information in the seat pocket in front of me, as the same nice lady said I should, so I know every emergency exit on every plane that has ever managed to go from Bangkok (which airlines insist on spelling as BKK) to Chiang Mai (which inexplicably turns into CNX).

Of course, this safety information card is truly a greater nonsense than some of our politicians' promises. Take a look, next time you have finished the stale sponge cake and nuts. First off there are wonderful artistic renditions of your downed aeroplane floating on the water, while the happy passengers, with their shoes removed, are getting into the inflatable life rafts on their way to salvation, or some other suitable port of call (hopefully duty free).

Have you ever stopped to wonder why they use artist's drawings and not the real thing? Well this is simple to answer. The mega-tonne plane will not float. It will sink. It has no provisions for landing on water, unless it is a seaplane, and they don't use those in either Bangkok (sorry, BKK) or CNX. The *klong*s (canals) are neither straight enough, wide enough nor long enough. Stricken aeroplanes break up on hitting the water at X hundred kilometres per hour. They do.

Have you ever seen a picture of a ditched plane that is sitting nonchalantly on top of the water, in one piece, and waiting for the happy shoeless passengers to return in their inflatable life rafts after their duty-free shopping splurge? Of course not. The damn things break into small sections and sink. To the bottom!

The cabin crew, who obviously all have a great sense of humour, do tell you about how to put on your life vest and how to pull the string and how it magically inflates. Mind you, they also are honest enough to tell you what to do when it doesn't inflate, and you should use the mouth tubes to complete the job, so you shouldn't really believe that some light on your shoulder is really going to work either after you have reached the water.

Now, when I have been in the situation of having to teach anybody anything, you get them to practice it, so that they can do it properly. If it is a matter of life and death, you get them to practice many times until they are completely proficient. Do the airlines give you a practice run? Do they hell! They just give you a sign on the back of the seat in front of you, that there really is a life vest (or 'live' vest) under your seat. Heaven help you if you have to find it after landing gently on the water. I just hope you remember how to tie it around your waist and put the hook in the rings and use your mouth tube and whistle. If you want a little fun, try pulling yours out from under your seat and practising with it, and see how long it is before you get pounced upon by the cabin crew. See what the nice lady does then!

No. When you hit the water, you may as well be resigned to the fact that you will be killed. Those who survive the initial impact will be lucky if they just drown. Or get eaten. It will be easier than trying to tie the loops through the rings while blowing your whistle to attract attention and inflate the thing with the mouth tubes. All I can think of is that you would have to have one helluva big mouth to do all that simultaneously!

But I almost forgot the real reason for this discourse. It's all apparent in the title—'terminally late'. That's at both terminals—departure and arrival! I have, so many times, stood waiting in the departure lounge (a euphemism for cattle corral) staring out at the naked end of the aero-bridge, because the plane isn't anywhere near the airport yet.

Forget about jostling at the barrier to get on first. There's no damn plane to get on to!

The end result of all this tardiness is that you are going to get to the other end even later than you are now. Unless you are in a Bell X 15 and able to fly at Mach 2. At last count none of the carriers had one of those, some preferring to use Boeing 747s that are older than I am.

There's a sign in the CNX arrival hall that says, 'We are ready to be the aviation hub of the region.' I have news for them. Until they can fly to a timetable, they're not ready! And that seems a long way off yet.

~

Cheers!

The Elixir of Life

MANY DAYS SOME EX-PAT WILL come into my office complaining about an aspect of their life in Thailand. I bite my tongue as the words, 'Well, why don't you go back to where you came from?' come to my mind.

What many foreigners forget while living here is that they are living in the country that many of their own countrymen save their money for 11 months a year just to be able to visit for two to four weeks. And we live here for 52 weeks each year! They should be laughing, not complaining.

I have to admit that every morning as I drive along Jomtien Beach Road on the way to the office I do burst out laughing. I am laughing at nobody, laughing from the sheer joy of living where I want to be. Rather than the question, 'Does Thailand have the elixir of life?' I am of the opinion that perhaps Thailand itself may be that much sought after elixir. There are many reasons for my proposition.

In my previous life in Australia I was a rather keen motor racer. Keen is an understatement—motor racing was my passion, but I had to retire from active competition because of crippling arthritis. I was prepared to suffer the ignominy of having to be extracted from the car by my pit crew at the end of a race, but when you have to be helped onto the podium to receive the spoils of victory this really means the end. I did retire at the top, having being helped by the officials to climb on to the top step!

I also had a lifelong affair with motorcycles, but had to give that up too, as I could not swing my leg over the saddle without excruciating pain in my hip. In Australia I was 56 years old, going on 65! The pathway seemed to be totally downhill. However, I had this dream of living in Thailand. By 1997 I had reached one of those forks in the road. Should I stay in Australia where I was considered to be reasonably affluent, or should I give it all up and pursue this dream of living in the mystic orient—Thailand?

My family history was not a good one. As I mention earlier, no male had ever reached his 57th birthday, all dying from heart attacks. My father had come the closest at 56 years, 11 months and 2 weeks before succumbing to his final cardiac catastrophe. I too was now 56. Was I to follow the family (mis)fortune as well? I played the scenario over in my mind—the option of staying in a country where I was now too infirm to follow the lifestyle I had enjoyed (and being in a country that was over-governed and over-policed in every way) and dying, saying on my death bed, 'But I wanted to live in Thailand!'

The second option was just to leave, before it was too late. The family cardiac clock was ticking loudly. I took the second option.

Like many others, I gave up much to come to Thailand, having made that fateful decision. Unable to sell my practice, I just closed the doors. Unable to sell the family home, I left it in the care of a relative, who after 12 months managed to reduce it in value to just marginally more than the amount owing on the mortgage. But I was doing something I had wanted to do for 22 years. I was living in Thailand. The land of my dreams.

I was in Pattaya as I came up to the 57 year family nemesis. The final two weeks took an eternity as I crawled past my father in years lived on terra firma. My 57th birthday would have to be one like no other before, and only Thailand could offer me the sort of birthday I chose, which was that unforgettable night on stage with the *katoeys*. .

On top of that, from a presumed future of cardiac incapacity, I was looking stronger than any male in my family's living (or dead) history!

After one year of living in Thailand I began to notice some other very distinct changes—not in Thailand, but in me. The arthritis was going. I could throw a leg over a motorcycle again. I could punt a race car around the Bira circuit without having to be physically dragged out of the car. There was only the occasional twinge in one finger of my left hand. From a presumed future of crippling arthritis I could run and jog again.

After four years of living in Thailand other changes became evident. A young Thai lady stole my heart. We dated, complete with chaperone, but I had to (secretly) agree with her family—I probably wouldn't have let my daughter out with me either, without a chaperone!

Life now began to change in earnest after six years of living in Thailand. My young lady and I made the fateful decision and we became a married couple (the full dramas in doing this have been the subject of another Thailand dissertation).

It is now ten years in the Kingdom and life has continued with the advent of my wife's first child, and my first daughter, followed by a son. A new life has been given to us to nurture, which in turn has meant a new life for me too. I am now 62 going on 26.

In retrospect, it looks as if Thailand really is the elixir of life. For me at least, it certainly is.

~

MISS BANGKOK

Memoirs of a Thai Prostitute

By BUA BOONMEE
WITH NICOLA PIERCE

Miss Bangkok is a vivid, powerful and moving memoir of a life spent in prostitution in Thailand. Poor and uneducated, Bua Boonmee escaped an abusive marriage only to end up in the go-go bars of Patpong. There, in the notorious red-light district of Bangkok, she succumbed to prostitution in an effort to support her family.

Bua's story is one of resilience and courage in the face of abuse and poverty. Her confessions will make you laugh and cry, cringe and applaud. She will change your perception of prostitution forever.

To order this book go to www.maverickhouse.com

THE LAST EXECUTIONER

Memoirs of Thailand's last Prison Executioner

By CHAVORET JARUBOON
WITH NICOLA PIERCE

Chavoret Jaruboon was personally responsible for executing 55 prison inmates on Thailand's infamous death row.

As a boy, he wanted to be a teacher like his father, then a rock'n'roll star like Elvis, but his life changed when he joined Thailand's prison service. From there he took on one of the hardest jobs in the world.

Honest and often disturbing—but told with surprising humour and emotion—*The Last Executioner* is the remarkable story of one man's experiences with life and death.

Emotional and at times confronting, the book grapples with the controversial topic of the death sentence and makes no easy reading.

This book is not for the faint hearted—*The Last Executioner* takes you right behind the bars of the Bangkok Hilton and into death row.

WELCOME TO HELL

One Man's Fight for Life inside
the 'Bangkok Hilton'

By COLIN MARTIN

Written from his cell and smuggled out page by page, Colin Martin's autobiography chronicles an innocent man's struggle to survive inside one of the world's most dangerous prisons.

After being swindled out of a fortune, Martin was let down by the hopelessly corrupt Thai police. Forced to rely upon his own resources, he tracked down the man who conned him and, drawn into a fight, accidentally stabbed and killed the man's bodyguard.

Martin was arrested, denied a fair trial, convicted of murder and thrown into prison—where he remained for eight years. Honest and often disturbing, *Welcome to Hell* is the remarkable story of how Martin was denied justice again and again.

In his extraordinary account, he describes the swindle, his arrest and vicious torture by police, the unfair trial, and the eight years of brutality and squalor he was forced to endure.

To order this book go to www.maverickhouse.com

THE ANGEL OF BANG KWANG PRISON

By SUSAN ALDOUS
WITH NICOLA PIERCE

The inmates of Bang Kwang Prison in Bangkok rarely have anything to look forward to; except a visit from their own personal angel.

Susan Aldous had been on a path of self-destruction when she decided to give her life to others instead of wasting it away in Melbourne's dark underbelly.

Realising she wanted to help the poorest of the poor, Susan moved to Singapore and then to Thailand to work on a nine-day project helping the socially disadvantaged. She is still there 18 years later.

A single mother with no salary and few possessions, she devotes her life to helping others, bringing hope and humanity to the prison; one of the toughest places on Earth, among other projects.

Whether it is teaching young Thai men to accept the world they live in, or helping foreign inmates adjust to life in a Thai jail, Susan Aldous is a one-woman charity phenomenon. There are 7,000 inmates in the prison; all of them have heard of Susan, the 'Angel of Bang Kwang'.

This is her story.

To order this book go to www.maverickhouse.com